D0398169

Get Anyone to Do Anything

Also by David J. Lieberman, Ph.D.

Instant Analysis
Never Be Lied to Again

Get Anyone to Do Anything

Never Feel Powerless Again—
WITH PSYCHOLOGICAL
SECRETS TO CONTROL AND
INFLUENCE EVERY SITUATION

David J. Lieberman, Ph.D.

 St. Martin's Griffin ⚉ New York

GET ANYONE TO DO ANYTHING. Copyright © 2000 by David J. Lieberman, Ph.D. All rights reserved. Printed in the United States of America. No part of this book may be used or reproduced in any manner whatsoever without written permission except in the case of brief quotations embodied in critical articles or reviews. For information, address St. Martin's Press, 175 Fifth Avenue, New York, N.Y. 10010.

www.stmartins.com

Library of Congress Cataloging-in-Publication Data

Lieberman, David J.
    Get anyone to do anything : never feel powerless again—
with psychological secrets to control and influence every situation. /
David J. Lieberman, Ph.D.
       p.   cm.
    Includes bibliographical references (p.181–184).
    ISBN 0-312-20904-5 (hc)
    ISBN 0-312-27017-8 (pbk)
    1. Psychology, Applied   I. Title.
BF636.L46   2000
158.2—dc21   00-027043
                                    CIP

10 9 8 7 6 5 4

Contents

Acknowledgments

I am grateful for the opportunity to acknowledge the pleasure I had in working with the outstanding professionals at St. Martin's Press.

First and foremost, I would like to thank executive editor Jennifer Enderlin. Every author should have the opportunity to work with someone so dedicated and talented. And to all those who have worked tirelessly, my warmest thanks to the publicity, marketing, advertising, and sales departments at St. Martin's for their intense efforts and commitment: Alison Lazarus, John Cunningham, Steve Kasdin, John Murphy, Jamie Brickhouse, Mike Storrings, Janet Wagner, Mark Kohut, Darin Keesler, Lynn Kovach, Jeff Capshew, and Ken Holland, and to the entire Broadway Sales Department for their continued efforts on behalf of this book.

A special thanks to St. Martin's publisher, Sally Richardson, for her continued enthusiasm for my work and this project. My appreciation also goes to Estelle Laurence, copy editor, for her outstanding work on the manuscript.

My deepest gratitude to my friend Rabbi Henry Harris for his invaluable input and suggestions; his wisdom is evident throughout this book. I would like to thank also my friends and agents, Michael Larsen and Elizabeth Pomada, for their outstanding contribution to this project.

Finally, this book cites numerous studies by remarkable psychologists who have devoted their lives to better understanding the human condition. It is because of them that this book is everything that it is.

Introduction

Are you tired of being manipulated and taken advantage of? Do you sometimes feel you're not being listened to and don't get the respect and cooperation that you deserve? If you've ever wanted the ability to take control of every conversation and situation, *now you've got it*! Why go through life letting others lead you, when you can use the greatest psychological secrets to make things go your way . . . get anyone to do anything . . . and never feel powerless again!

Here, you enter a world where psychology reigns and detecting deceit, changing a person's mind, or controlling a situation are reduced to an easy-to-follow formula—a series of simple techniques and tactics.

You will be able to use the most complete and advanced psychological strategies to enable your mind to become your greatest weapon. Most exciting, you should know that we're not talking about "tricks" that work *sometimes* on *some people*. This book contains *only specific psychological tactics governing human behavior* that will let you outsmart, outthink, and outmaneuver . . . *anyone, anyplace, anytime*. These are carefully formulated tactics based on specific psychological principles and can be applied to *any* situation.

Imagine how easy life would be if you were able to predict and control the outcome of any encounter. And instead of wondering what was going to happen, you applied proven, fast-working psychological tactics to gain complete and total cooperation from all people in any situation.

Have you ever asked someone to help you out and much to your surprise she happily obliged? Or perhaps you wanted to make a good impression and the person found you completely irresistible? You wonder if it was luck, the person's mood, or the situation—when in actuality you likely applied principles that govern human behavior without even knowing it. The good news is that you can *duplicate* those same responses, *systematically,* any time you want, with anyone.

To make it easy for you to learn how to apply these psychological secrets, the book is divided into forty mini-chapters, each governing various real-life situations. And best of all, once you become familiar with the psychological principles, you'll see that you can use the techniques to be successful anytime, in *any* situation that you find yourself in.

Get ready to make life easy and have things go *your* way, when you . . . *Get Anyone to Do Anything . . . and Never Feel Powerless Again*!

The Secrets Inside and How to Use Them

THE GREATEST COLLECTION OF PSYCHOLOGICAL TACTICS TO MAKE EVERYTHING GO *YOUR* WAY

If you wanted to make life easy what would be on your wish list? Maybe . . . in every area of life you know how to avoid ever being taken advantage of or manipulated; are able to end verbal conflicts with a single phrase; understand how to lead, influence, and motivate anyone to your way of thinking; and are able to become anything to anyone by winning friends and changing instantly how others see you. In short, you'd have a life made easy. You're about to learn how to use the greatest psychological techniques for success *in every area of your life*.

SECTION I: GET ANYONE TO LIKE YOU, LOVE YOU, OR JUST PLAIN THINK YOU'RE GREAT!

If you want to be successful in life, you often need to get cooperation from other people. And the number-one rule for getting people to do what you want is to get them to *like you*. Whether you want to make a new friend or gain an ally, these psychological tactics show you step-by-step how to get anyone to think you're great. Plus, in romantic situations you'll discover how to get anyone to find you irresistibly attractive. And, once you're in the relationship, you'll be able to apply the greatest secrets for *always* having the upper hand.

SECTION II: NEVER BE FOOLED, TRICKED, MANIPULATED, USED, LIED TO, OR TAKEN ADVANTAGE OF AGAIN

If you want to make life go your way, you, of course, want to avoid being manipulated and fooled by people who don't have your best interests at heart. You would need to "see through people" and easily tell who is out *for you* and who is out to *get you*. In this section you'll learn psychological tactics to determine, almost instantly, if someone is trying to take advantage of you. Whether it's personal or professional, you never have to get that helpless feeling of trusting the wrong person again.

SECTION III: TAKE CONTROL OF ANY SITUATION AND GET ANYONE TO DO ANYTHING

Now, to really make things go your way, you're going to need to control certain situations. Here you'll learn how to easily influence others to your way of thinking. Get anyone to understand, agree with, and then do what you want! Learn the secrets to getting a single person or an entire group to trust, believe, and follow you. Whether it's changing one person's opinion or leading a crowd, you'll use the latest and most advanced tools governing human nature to *make people go your way*.

SECTION IV: HOW TO WIN AT ANY COMPETITION: BEAT OUT ANYONE FOR THE JOB, FOR THE DATE, OR FOR THE GAME

Sometimes it's not a matter of swaying a person to *your side*—when, for instance, you are *competing* with someone for the *same thing*. You'll learn the greatest psychological techniques for winning at any competition. Whether it's a tennis match, a job promotion, or even a date, when it's *you* against *him, you'll win*. In this section you'll learn how to make your mind your greatest weapon and become the perfect psychological warrior.

SECTION V: MAKE LIFE EASY: LEARN HOW TO INSTANTLY TAKE LIFE'S MOST ANNOYING, FRUSTRATING, AND DIFFICULT SITUATIONS AND GET THE UPPER HAND EVERY TIME!

Wouldn't it be great if everyone was as nice and pleasant as you? Sure it would, but some people aren't and they just get "under our skin." So, for life's little nuisances this section gives you an array of tactics where a little psychology goes a long way. Whether you want a phone call returned or you want someone to forgive you, these techniques work to *make life easy*!

Note to readers: Because these techniques are based on human nature, factors such as culture, race, and gender are negligible, unless otherwise noted. Throughout all of the examples in this book the pronouns *he* and *she* are used interchangeably. This was done to make the language less sexist, not to indicate that the technique is gender specific.

GET ANYONE TO LIKE YOU, LOVE YOU, OR JUST PLAIN THINK YOU'RE GREAT!

Here you will discover those psychological factors that *influence the levels of interest* other people have in you. You're going to see just how easy it is for you to get anyone to like you (or dislike you). By following a simple strategy based on human nature, you can create trusting, lasting friendships and relationships with complete ease. And so we're clear, these aren't ways to *manipulate* other people into liking you. Rather, you'll be orchestrating the application of certain psychological principles and methodologies to bring out and develop a *natural chemistry*.

The obvious question then is, "Why do I need these techniques if all I'm doing is bringing out a natural chemistry? Doesn't it stand to reason that if it's there it's there, and if it's not it's not?" While that seems as if it would be so, below explains why the answer is no.

It is in our nature as human beings to seek affiliation, to make friends, and to care about others. But sometimes it can be hard for a person to reach out and "expose" his or her true self and feelings. Most people want to like, want to love, want to connect, but they are afraid. Things get in the way of their innate desire; things like fear of rejection, vulnerability, ego, and jealousy are but a few of the multitude of mixed emotions, attitudes, and beliefs that keep us from reaching out and bonding with others. What these psychological techniques do is to simply *influence a person's natural state to emerge.* We feel good when we *give,* when we *love,* and when we *help.* It's not about twisting someone's brain so that he does your unconditional bidding; it's about bringing the person's submerged desires to the surface.

In this section we cover different levels of interpersonal relations. At the core of all relationships, though, is *mutual liking*. No one will be attracted (for any length of time) to someone whom he doesn't *like* and *respect*. So, the tactics below, while separated into individual specific strategies, *can and should be used together*. Most important, Chapter 1, Get Anyone to Like You . . . Every Time, is the foundation not only for this section but for several of the chapters throughout the book. We'll talk more about the importance of this later.

1

Get Anyone to Like You . . . Every Time

What are those elusive traits and qualities that arouse feelings of friendship and likability in a person? In just a minute you'll discover that they're not elusive at all. In fact they can be reduced to a simple formula that will help you to develop a natural chemistry with anyone.

The fact is we like or dislike a person based upon a strict set of mostly unconscious processes. It does not happen by chance. But the reality that we're unaware of the process makes it *seem* as if it occurs without much rhyme or reason. Nothing could be farther from the truth. The following is a complete list and discussion of the nine psychological laws and phenomena that *affect, influence,* and even *alter* what we think of someone so you can *get anyone to like you.*

Keep in mind, too, that research shows that our liking a person can influence how physically attractive we think he or she is, and that we also tend to *like more* someone whom we find attractive. So this chapter and the one that follows it go hand-in-hand and can be used as part of an overall strategy.

1. Law of Association

The law of association is discussed in more detail throughout this book, but it has a very specific application here. Briefly, by pairing yourself with pleasurable stimuli another person will begin to associate you with this feeling. Studies conclude that if, for instance, you were planning your vacation you would associate those favorable feelings with whoever was around you at the time, and you would subsequently like the person more. Conversely, research in this area shows us that when you have a stomachache, for instance, those around you become unconscious victims of circumstance, and you tend to *like them less*. Of course there's more to liking than just this pairing of pleasant stimuli with a person, but it can generate powerful feelings, either good or bad, toward you.

So if you want to be liked by a person, try talking to him when he is in a *good mood* or *excited* about something. These feelings are anchored and associated with you, and this person will then come to have positive feelings toward you.

Power Point

Sometimes it's easy to tell if a person's in a good mood. But if you're not sure, *look at his face*.

⇨ If he's in a good mood he'll likely greet you with a full smile, eyes wide open. If he greets you with a partial "lips only" smile—one that does not involve his whole face—then this is a "forced courtesy smile" and usually reflects a person who is not in a good mood.

⇨ Eye contact is a strong indicator of mood. When we are in a good mood we tend to make *more direct eye contact*. Conversely, when we're in a bad mood we tend to look down or away from the person we're speaking to.

---

2. REPEAT EXPOSURE

The old adage "familiarity breeds contempt" is commonly accepted but interestingly enough, *it's not true*. In reality, it's the opposite. Numerous studies conclude that the *more* you interact with someone, the *more* he or she will like you.

According to Moreland and Zajonc (1982), repeated exposure to any stimulus—in this case a person—leads to a greater appreciation and liking (as long as the initial reaction is not negative). This is true of anything—a person, a place, or even a product: *the greater the exposure, the more positive the response*. This is why companies sometimes advertise *just a picture* of a product, or *its name*, without any specific features or benefits of using the product. They don't need to tell us how wonderful it is, only *remind us* of it. Exposure, being an obvious component of repetition, can alone increase sales or votes, which is why advertisers and politicians exploit this phenomenon. This factor of human behavior is so powerful that studies show that *even a letter in the alphabet* that also appears in our name is perceived as *more attractive* than a letter that is not in our name.

By simply being around more, you will actually "grow" on this person. Sometimes we make the mistake of trying to appear mysterious, aloof, or unavailable to someone, but in doing so we diminish our number of interactions. Studies conclude that we become friends with, and tend to like more, those who are physically nearest to us because of this increased level of interaction. (By the way, you don't have to worry about enacting the *law of scarcity,* unless you want this person to be *attracted to you!* That is because the basis of liking follows a different paradigm than for attraction. We will learn more about that law in this section.)

3. RECIPROCAL AFFECTION

Countless studies (and common sense) have established that we tend to like more those who like us. When we find out that someone thinks well of us, we in turn are unconsciously driven to find him or her more likable as well. Therefore, you want to let your "target person" know that you *like* and *respect him,* if indeed you do.

 Power Point

What if he really doesn't like me at all? Oddly enough, studies conclude that *if he started out not liking you and gradually came around to liking you, he will eventually like you more than if he had liked you right from the beginning.* Keep in mind, if you don't have a great relationship with him, *don't do a "180,"* suddenly making this person your best friend. Studies show us that *gradual liking* is infinitely more effective than instantly becoming someone's best friend. So don't be overwhelming and "out-of-the-blue" his number-one fan. To engage the law of reciprocal affection *gradually,* let it be known that you are fond of this person.

---

4. SIMILARITIES

It is not true that opposites attract. We actually like more those people who are similar to us and who have similar interests. We may find someone interesting because of how different he is from us, but it's the *similarities* and *commonalities* that generate mutual liking. *Like attracts like.* When you speak to this person, *talk about what you both enjoy* and what you have in *common*.

Similar to this law is the principle of "comrades in arms." Essentially, people who go through life-changing situations together tend to create a significant bond. For instance, soldiers in battle or those in fraternity pledge classes who get hazed together usually develop strong friendships. This is also a powerful bonding method even if the experience was not shared, but *similarly experienced*. It's for this reason that two people who have never met but who have shared a similar previous experience—whether it's an illness or winning the lottery—can become instant friends. It is the "she understands me" perspective that generates these warm feelings for another who has had a similar experience. It all comes down to the fact that we all want to be understood, and this powerful event has likely helped to shape the person into who she is today; hence this other person "knows and understands" what she is all about.

5. HOW YOU MAKE HER FEEL

How someone feels about you is greatly determined by how you make her feel about herself. You can spend all day trying to get her to like you and to think well of you, but it's how *you make her feel* when she is around you that makes the difference. Have you ever noticed how nice it is to be around someone who is complimentary and sincerely kind and warm? Conversely, have you ever thought about how annoying it is to spend five minutes with the person who's always finding fault with everything and everyone? These people seem to drain the life right out of you. Being the person who makes people *feel good* will go a long way toward their finding you quite likable.

6. Rapport

Rapport creates trust, allowing you to build a *psychological bridge* to someone. The conversation is likely to be more positive and comfortable when two people are "in sync" with each other. Just as we tend to like someone who shares our interests, we are also unconsciously driven to like a person when she "appears as we do." This means that when someone makes gestures the way we do, or uses words or phrases as we do, we tend to find him likable. More on rapport-building skills is discussed throughout various chapters in the book. For now, two powerful tips for establishing and building rapport are:

- *Matching posture and movements:* For instance, if someone has one hand in his pocket, you put your hand in yours. If he makes a gesture with his hand, after a moment and without being obvious, you casually make the same gesture.
- *Matching speech:* Try to match his rate of speech. If he's speaking in a slow, relaxed tone, you do the same. If he's speaking quickly, then you begin to speak more rapidly.

7. Helping Her Out

Studies in human nature show us that people dislike others more after doing them harm. Please note that I did not say that *we do harm to those whom we dislike,* although this may be true. The point here is that when we do harm to another, either on purpose or by accident, *we are unconsciously driven to dislike the person.* This is an attempt to reduce dissonance. (Cognitive dissonance theory as it applies here states that we feel uneasy when we do something that is inconsistent with how we see ourselves. Therefore to reduce this inner conflict we rationalize our actions to remain consistent with our self-concept.) The internal conflict created is, "Why did I do this to this person?" The rationalization then becomes, "It must be because I really don't like him and he deserves it. Otherwise I would be a bad or careless person, and that cannot be so." *This works in reverse as well.* We like someone *more* after doing something nice for him or her. If we do someone a favor we are likely to have positive feelings toward that person.

If you can get him to *do you* a small favor, this will generate kind and warm feelings toward you. Often, in our attempt to get someone to like us, we make the mistake of doing nice things for him. And while he may appreciate your kindness and think you're a nice person, *it doesn't make him like you more,* even though you may be viewed as more likable. What you want is for him to have kind feelings toward you, not to just believe that you are a kind person. This is accomplished by *him doing for you,* not by you doing for him.

8. HE'S ONLY HUMAN

Seeing someone you admire do something stupid or clumsy will make you like him more (Aronson, Willerman, and Floyd, 1966). Contrary to popular belief, being a perfect, confident figure will *not* produce the desired outcome—meaning that it rarely leads to your being liked more and thought of in a positive way. When you want to be seen as more likable, do something embarrassing and *smile at yourself.* Don't try to ignore it or pretend it didn't happen. Self-deprecating humor is a terrific way to ingratiate yourself with anyone.

When you show others that you don't take yourself so seriously, it makes them feel closer to you and want to be around you. "Nobody likes a show-off" or a person who is so consumed with himself and his image that he needs to pretend that he is perfect. We tend to like and gravitate toward those who are not self-absorbed and egotistical. Showing that you can laugh at yourself makes you infinitely more approachable and likable. This is often at odds with what we think we should do. In our attempt to appear as "cool" and "important," others perceive us as taking ourselves too seriously, and this air of "false confidence" can be quite unbecoming.

This aspect of human nature confuses many people because the fact is that *we do like confident people;* we're drawn to and like those who are self-assured. But we know that a person who is confident doesn't feel the need to let the world know how great he is; he lets the world find out for itself. So the bragging, arrogant person *is really a person who feels small inside* and we are often instinctively uninterested and unattracted to this person. The one who is confident and secure is the one who is apt to laugh at his own mistakes and is not afraid to let people know that he is human. So you see, they are not at conflict with one another. Not taking ourselves so seriously and acknowledging our faults and mistakes *shows the world that we are confident.*

9. POSITIVE ATTITUDE

As we talked about before, we like people who are similar to us. But there is one exception to this rule. *Nobody wants to be around a moody, often pissed-off, pessimistic person.* We all seek, like, and admire those who have a positive, happy outlook and perspective on life. Why? Because that is what we all want. And seeing this desirable spirit in others makes us like them more. You may know a person—or may even be someone—who finds annoying those who wake up smiling and in a good mood. The fact is though, at some level we are *drawn* to that attitude and to that person. Think of the people in your life whom you really can't stand to be around. Chances are they are always complaining about something; always annoyed with somebody; always finding fault with everything. Like confidence, a positive attitude toward life will help to turn you into a superhuman magnet for attracting people and getting anyone to like you.

But wait a minute! Doesn't misery love company? Actually it does. Miserable people like to be around others who are just as annoyed with life as they are. But this quality *does not* make them *like* these people more. Someone who feels miserable enjoys commiserating and complaining with another miserable individual, but the minute he's in a good mood he will abandon the toxic, annoying person. He seeks solace with somebody who feels as he does, but when he no longer feels that way he will instantly leave this relationship. This is because he never liked the person (at least not for this similarity); he enjoyed only the shared attitude.

Strategy Review

🖋 Be around the person as much as you can because familiarity breeds *fondness*, not contempt!

🖋 When you speak with him try to do it when he's in a *good mood* to enact the law of association. Talk about *common in-*

terests or experiences that you share and try to do more of the *listening* and less of the talking.

- To enact the law of reciprocal affection, if you *respect* or *admire* him for something make sure that he knows this.

- *Let him do a simple favor for you,* but make sure that it's not out of a sense of obligation. This creates an unconscious motivation to like you more.

- Build a psychological bridge and establish rapport by matching the person's gestures, rate of speech, and vocal patterns.

- We are drawn to confident people. Show your confidence by being able to laugh at yourself and *not taking yourself too seriously.*

- Make her feel good about herself. Be someone who is complimentary and sincerely kind and warm.

- Have a positive mental attitude. We are drawn to people who are excited, passionate, and happy about life and being alive.

- See Chapter 2, Get Anyone to Find You Irresistibly Attractive, because we tend to like more those whom we find attractive— same sex or not.

2

Get Anyone to Find You Irresistibly Attractive

While we all have different physical preferences, these tactics will greatly help you to maximize your "assets" and in most cases override another person's basic idea of what he finds attractive. How can this be done? Have you ever dated someone who was not even close to your type? Why'd you do it? Because he or she enacted these laws, most likely unwittingly, and you found that person simply irresistible.

If you want to be appealing to anyone, use the techniques in the previous chapter and then move on to those in this chapter for maximum success. Numerous studies as well as real life show us that the more we like someone the more attractive we tend to find him or her. Although the tactics outlined below are especially designed for romantic interest, it should be said that we rarely find attractive those whom we do not like. So, fold into your game plan the tactics in the preceding chapter to give you an unstoppable overall strategy.

1. Emotion Arousal

This single tactic will be responsible for getting you more dates than any hairstyle or outfit or high-powered job ever will. It is a foundation of human behavior that when our body produces *adrenaline,* feelings of *attraction* to those present and *sexual desire* often result. Adrenaline, produced through any state of heightened arousal—fear, excitement, exercise, or whatever—*generates* and *intensifies passionate feelings.* (This assumes that attraction exists in some form, at some level.)

Anytime a person is aroused, such as with scary movies, amusement park rides, or even physical exercise, his arousal will in part be attributed to whomever he is with. In effect, there is a transference of state where the excitement he feels gets unconsciously translated into sexual desire and arousal. The next time you see a couple who appears to be "aesthetically" mismatched, ask where they met. Chances are good that they met under circumstances where arousal was high . . . maybe at the gym or while one person (the better-looking of the two) was apprehensive, nervous, or excited about something.

 Power Point

It's for this very fact that psychologists are becoming increasingly disturbed by the trend—in video games, movies, and television—of associating *violence* and *sex*. The pairing of these two stimuli—sexual content and violence—can generate enhanced arousal toward violence and aggressive tendencies in sexual encounters.

---

2. WALKING STYLES

Youth is often deemed to be a factor of physical attractiveness. But the good news is that you don't necessarily have to *look* young but merely *appear* young. Even something as seemingly innocuous as posture and how a person walks plays a powerful role in how youthful we judge him. Walking styles definitely influence physical attractiveness. People react more favorably to those whose walking style seems youthful than to those who seem elderly, *regardless of the actual age or sex* (Montepare and Zebrowitz-McArthur, 1988). What exactly determines youthful posture and gait? *Flexibility.* Observe a small child, and note how flexible she is in comparison to an elderly person. Yoga will greatly improve your flexibility and will make a dramatic difference in your overall posture, walking style, and how attractive others perceive you to be.

Power Point

There are several popular theories on why we are attracted to youth. The most widely accepted is that this is a biological instinct courtesy of our ancestors. Women who have youthful features are likely to be of childbearing age—considered a desirable state by men. Men who are young are perceived as more virile, considered as good protectors and providers by women for them and their children.

3. GAZING INTO A PERSON'S EYES

Did you know that gazing into a person's eyes can actually make the individual fall in love with you? That's the conclusion of numerous studies on attraction and romantic love. In one particular experiment, two opposite-sex strangers were asked to gaze into each other's eyes for two minutes. This study concluded that the act of simply looking into another's eyes for only a few moments was enough for them to produce *passionate feelings for each other* (Kellerman, Lewis, and Laird, 1989).

To make use of this tactic when you have a *conversation* with this person, look him directly in the eyes when *speaking* and *listening*. Most of the time we sort of gaze generally at a person's face or divert our glance when in conversation. By looking into his eyes, while speaking with him, you engage this psychological phenomenon without being obvious.

4. THE LAW OF CONTRAST AND ASSOCIATION

When you want someone to find you attractive your best bet is to meet this person initially *by yourself* or with you being accompanied by an *attractive person of the opposite sex*. This is because of the *law of contrast* and the *law of association*.

We don't often judge a person by herself, but in *contrast* with other people. This is intensified when it comes to meeting someone for the first time. We see and think of her physical attributes in *comparison* to those she is with. There have been many studies in this area, including some that confirm that men who have recently been looking at bathing suit models find other women—or even their own wives—less attractive.

Herein lies one of the biggest mistakes we often make. Before someone has a chance to know the real you, and to be influenced by these other tactics, your physical beauty is the first thing you're judged by. So put the odds in your favor. Do not, I repeat, *do not* find yourself in the company of those who are more attractive than you (of the same sex) when you want someone to become interested in you.

When meeting this person, generally for the first time only, try also not to be in the company of terribly unattractive people, *of either sex*. This is because of the *law of association*—where we tend to see a group as a whole and not the individuals.

Therefore, again, your best approach is to be *by yourself* or with an attractive person of the opposite sex. This will also afford you the opportunity to use your other tactics without distraction. (The reason you can be with an attractive person of the opposite sex is that the law of association takes precedence over the law of contrast when the members of the group are more different than they are similar. In other words, your attractiveness is enhanced by this person because you are seen as "one unit.")

5. Self-Esteem and Attraction

This is a tactic to use if your own beauty is limited, as it will allow you to be seen initially as much more attractive than you might otherwise appear.

A study by Elaine Walster Hatfield showed that a woman who is introduced to a man will find him *more appealing* if her self-esteem has been temporarily injured than a woman whose self-esteem has not been impaired (Walster Hatfield, 1965). While you wouldn't want to go out of your way to make someone feel bad about herself, should you become aware that this person has recently had a rejection, you should know you would appear to be more attractive to her than if her self-esteem were in high gear. This law is what is responsible for the good old *rebound effect* whereby a person finds herself fast into a relationship right after one ends, usually with someone whom she wouldn't under "normal conditions" date.

Another way to "slip in under the radar" is to simply approach her when she is with other more attractive people. Studies conclude that when we're around people who we feel are better-looking than we are, we tend to feel less confident about ourselves and our appearance. Again, when our own self-esteem is suffering we tend to view others as more attractive.

So when the person is feeling less than good about herself, be flirtatious and friendly. The caveat here is the law of human nature that says *people want what they can't have* and they *like more what they have to work for.* So prevent this law from hurting you by not being too obvious. Be interested and attentive but not overly so. This is discussed at greater length later in this section when we talk specifically about relationships and getting the upper hand.

6. RECIPROCAL LIKING

We touched on this in the previous chapter, but it is included here because this law also impacts on us at a *romantic level.* Studies have shown that when we find out that someone we like finds us appealing, it actually awakens romantic feelings within us. Again, not only do we like those who like us, but we're also more *attracted* to those people once we learn that they are *attracted* to us. This is because an essential aspect of passionate feelings is *hope.* If the other person has absolutely no interest in you then you may find her attractive but *not develop a real and intense attraction* and *desire.* Hope paves the way for stronger, more intense romantic feelings. And finding out that someone likes us gives us hope that a relationship is possible and will intensify our feelings toward him or her.

Strategy Review

- Engage in an activity with this person where *emotional arousal is high.*
- The perception of youth increases attraction. Your *posture* and *walking style* influence greatly how youthful you appear.
- Passionate feelings for another can easily develop by simply staring into someone's eyes. Look her directly in the eyes when *speaking* and *listening.*

🖊 We find others *more attractive* at those times when we feel less confident about ourselves. Approaching her when she feels self-conscious will make you appear more attractive.

🖊 Once she already likes you, *deepen the attraction* by letting her know that you are attracted to her.

🖊 Review the techniques in Chapter 1, Get Anyone to Like You . . . Every Time. Then once the relationship gets going make sure you follow the techniques in Chapter 5, Get Anyone to See You as Pure Gold, to keep the passion strong. But, before you do, don't forget if you haven't already met you're going to want to make the best first impression possible. So let's go to Chapter 3, How to Make a Fantastic First Impression, which gives you even more psychological techniques to round out your overall strategy.

3

How to Make a Fantastic First Impression

You never have to worry again about how you're going to come across, because when you apply these psychological secrets, you'll be able to make the very best first impression, *every time.* Whether in personal or professional situations, these secrets will give you the winning edge over your competition. Remember that these techniques and Chapter 1, Get Anyone to Like You . . . Every Time, work in complementary fashion; review both in order to have all of your psychological weapons in line so you can carefully devise your strategy.

The number-one tactic for generating a favorable first impression is the easiest to do: *Smile!* Smiling accomplishes four powerful things: It conveys *confidence, happiness,* and *enthusiasm,* and most important, it shows *acceptance.* People who smile are perceived as *confident* because when we are nervous or unsure about ourselves or our surroundings we tend not to smile. Smiling, of course, conveys *happiness* and we are drawn to happy people: We simply view them more favorably. Enthusiasm is essential to making a good impression because it's *contagious.* Your smile shows that you are pleased to be where you are and to meet this person and he in turn becomes more interested in meeting you. Finally, smiling conveys *acceptance* and lets the other person know that you unconditionally accept who he or she is. Have you ever wondered why dogs are so lovable? Because they greet us with complete acceptance. If you have a tail, then wag it. If you don't, then smile. Of course there's more to ensuring a good first impression, so let's continue.

Regarding first impressions, there is something called the *primacy effect:* the process whereby our first impression of another person causes us to interpret his or her subsequent behavior in a manner consistent with the first impression. In English, this means that our first impression of someone is *so crucial* because everything we see and hear *afterward* gets filtered through our initial opinion. In effect you create an image of the person right when you meet him and you see his subsequent behaviors through this image. So *if his first impression of you is favorable then he will tend to be kinder in his future evaluations of you.*

The importance of primacy is so significant that even the *order of information* that we receive about somebody alters our impression of him. Take a look at these two lists of words.

A. Cold person, industrious, critical, practical, and determined

B. Warm person, industrious, critical, practical, and determined

In this study by Harold Kelley (1950), students who read the description of an upcoming guest lecturer on list *A* had a harsher perception of him than those who read from list *B*. As you can see, the words are identical, except for the *first one*. Once we read the first word all of the other qualities are filtered through our initial perception of this person: that he is either *warm* or *cold.*

Make that *initial moment* the very best and the rest of your conversation will be filtered through it, thereby creating a highly favorable impression. Again, that is why smiling is so important. You can do it right away and it says so much about you—and all positive.

Another factor that can dramatically influence how we are initially perceived is that of *accessibility and priming.* Simply, it's been clearly demonstrated that the *ease* with which we can recall certain thoughts and ideas colors our perception.

In a study showing just this (Higgins, Rholes, and Jones, 1977), those who had memorized the words *reckless, conceited, aloof,* and *stubborn* later formed negative impressions of a fictitious person. They viewed him as arrogant and as a person who needlessly took dangerous chances. However, people who first memorized the words *adventurous, self-confident, independent,* and *persistent* later formed positive impressions. Again, this is because these words and their corresponding ideas—what they represent—*were in the front of their minds.* And this colored their perception of a person whom they were "introduced" to for the very first time. Even though these words had *nothing to do with the person,* these qualities were "easily accessible" in the people's minds and they hence unconsciously ascribed those traits to somebody whom they then met.

So if you want to make a favorable impression on someone, it would benefit you if that person were to be recently exposed to *positive words.* If you're a job applicant your résumé should be peppered with positive adjectives (e.g., assertive, energetic, decisive, passionate, resourceful). Instead of just saying who you are and what you are capable of, use *strong, specific,* and *positive* language to convey precisely your talents and capabilities. Then when the interviewer meets you, shortly after reading through your résumé, these traits are already *"primed" for association with you.* (For another interesting application of the power of language see Chapter 26, The Best Way to Break Bad News.)

 Power Point

One of the biggest mistakes criminal defense attorneys make is to put their client on the stand when the details of the crime are still "fresh" and easily accessible in the minds of jurors. The better tactic is to put a witness or expert on the stand who uses *positive* and *trusting* language *immediately prior* to putting their client on the stand.

In personal as well as business situations you also want to lay the unconscious groundwork before you're introduced. Having a sales associate or your assistant tell your prospect about a recent vacation or a story that uses *positive, uplifting* language can be quite effective prior to your introduction. For instance, she might incorporate phrases such as, "beautiful view of this majestic scene . . . felt completely at peace and such a sense of calm . . . and security." This puts these themes directly in the mind of your prospect.

Personal situations offer more of a challenge, as introducing a third party isn't always practical. One way to circumvent this is to introduce these words directly yourself in the beginning of the conversation. Even though you don't get the benefit of the primacy effect, you'll recall from Chapter 1, Get Anyone to Like You . . . Every Time, the powerful influencing factor of association. These words will "rub off" onto you and will be *unconsciously associated with you.*

 Power Point

Who says you can't get a second chance at a first impression? If you did something incredibly inappropriate or stupid, *do not* try to defend your behavior. There's only one thing that will work: the phrase, "I feel so embarrassed." Why? Because this one phrase accomplishes *three* very important things. First, it shows that you know what you did was unacceptable—which means that you're unlikely to do it again. Second, it shows that you're human and people actually like us more when we acknowledge something stupid and embarrassing and then take responsibility for it. Third, it shows complete honesty—and who doesn't want to deal with an honest person?

Strategy Review

- *Smile!* Smiling accomplishes four powerful things: It conveys *confidence, happiness,* and *enthusiasm,* and most important, it shows *acceptance.*
- Engage the primacy effect and make that *initial moment* (and the first five minutes or so) the very best and the rest of your conversation will be filtered through it, thereby creating a highly favorable impression.
- The psychological phenomenon of *accessibility and priming* can dramatically influence how we are initially perceived. Lay the unconscious groundwork *prior* to your meeting.

4

Get the *Instant* Advantage in *Every* Relationship

The Four Biggest Mistakes and How to Avoid Them

You hate playing games, I know. But you're playing them anyway, so you might as well win. Whether it's business or personal the rules are the same to gain the upper hand *in any relationship.*

When dating, have you wondered why it seems it's the ones that you don't really like whom you can't seem to get rid of and the ones you *do* like who never seem to stick around? The reason is simple. It's *not* the person but the way you *behave* toward him or her.

What determines interest in another human being is a fascinating thing. Most people are actually on the fence at the start of most relationships. This means that almost every time someone can be swayed toward either liking or disliking you. And he is moved in either direction—either closer or farther—depending on how *you relate to him.*

This is because as human beings we are forever guided and governed by human nature. The bottom line is that it's not the person you're dating, *it's the things you are doing* that determine his or her level of interest. Otherwise it would be a startling coincidence if not a statistical improbability that everyone you liked just happened to "not want a commitment" and everyone you weren't that interested in wanted to marry you. So if it's not you—defined as your looks, personality, background, and so on—it must be *your behavior toward this person* that determines the direction and, ultimately, the outcome of the relationship.

This very powerful, yet simple psychological strategy can be summed up in one sentence: *You need to behave with the person you don't like the way you've been behaving with the person you do like, and vice versa.* While there are many little aspects of one's behavior, there are *four main factors,* which are discussed below.

AVAILABILITY

People want what they can't have. By constantly making yourself available, you're actually diminishing your value. This is not a trick or a game to play, but a function of human behavior. Attraction is not a fixed value. *This means that what someone thinks about you is determined to a large extent by what you do, not by just who you are or what you look like.* The law of scarcity is prevalent and relevant in every area of our lives, especially here. That which is plentiful is often underappreciated and that which is rare is held in high regard and considered valuable. When you are dating someone whom you are not that interested in, you tend to make yourself available when it's *convenient* for you. And when you're dating someone who you really like you're *consistently available.* Do the reverse!

This means when you're dating someone you don't like too much, if you're not baking cookies for him, calling him twice a day, asking where the relationship is going, and so on, *then don't do it with the person you like.* And by the way, when you do this with the ones you don't like, they'll be scared off soon enough, so you've eliminated this problem as well.

But wait! In Chapter 1, Get Anyone to Like You . . . Every Time, we said that if you want someone to like you, you *want to make yourself available,* because this increases liking. If this is so, doesn't it contradict the *law of scarcity*? Here's what is often misunderstood. If you want someone to like you, then you do indeed want to be in their company fairly often. This is true, but remember that *liking* is the foundation for every relationship. That means that once you *move past* the liking stage (meaning the person is already fond of you) and the relationship unfolds into something more serious, you *then* want to limit your availability.

Power Point

Here's a question. Don't we often see good-looking people with at-tractive partners and vice versa? If attraction has little to do with ap-pearance then why is this so? It's because *we are often most comfortable with those of similar levels of attractiveness.* (This coincides with studies that show that people are generally friends with those of similar levels of attractiveness.) A good-looking person can sometimes make a less attractive person feel uncomfortable. So this less attractive person tends to lose perspective *and act differently*—meaning that she puts the person on a pedestal and does the four things outlined in this chapter that she shouldn't be doing. But it's *the things* that she's doing—not her—the physical person—that make the difference. This is validated by the fact that sometimes attractive people *are* with less attractive people. In these relationships it's likely that the less attractive person feels confident about the relationship and hence *behaves* differently than their less attractive counterparts. (This "confidence" is replicated here when we apply the four factors to gaining leverage in the rela-tionship.)

PERSPECTIVE

In your relationships, you need perspective. In life, when we derive pleasure from only one source we tend to *overemphasize* its value and importance. You should find meaning in your life outside of the relationship so this person doesn't become your whole world. It's im-portant to feel fulfilled in other areas of your life so you're able to maintain a sensible perspective and not rely on someone else's affec-tions as your sole source of satisfaction and happiness. When you're dating someone you're not too interested in, you have plenty of per-spective because you're not thinking, "This is the only person for me; if I don't have him my world is over." You're thinking, "All right, let's see what happens; maybe he'll grow on me, and maybe he won't." And it's precisely that mentality that translates into the best attitude. And it's this attitude and your corresponding *behavior* that actually *make you more attractive.*

Passion

Here's the crux of how and why relationships work or fail. Simply, you can't appreciate what you take for granted. This is essentially why people, in general, become unhappy in their own lives. They always want more but are never grateful for what they have. And if you are not grateful for what you have, you will begin to take it for granted. And when you do this, you no longer appreciate it. And when you don't appreciate something it holds no enjoyment for you.

The same holds true for relationships. If someone takes you for granted he or she will not appreciate you and will begin to look for someone else. Similarly, if you went to the doctor and were told that you might lose your hearing, you would probably develop a renewed appreciation for sound.

Our gratitude lies in being reminded that we should not take these things for granted. And you don't take for granted what you believe can be taken away from you at any time. Similarly, if the object of your affections is a bit insecure with the relationship—meaning there is an element of *doubt*—then his or her lack of confidence will not lead to arrogance and ingratitude. *You must create an element of uncertainty or you will lose the passion that drives the relationship.*

 Power Point

Since it's possible for someone to be taken away from us at any time—by accident, by illness—why do you have to create *more* doubt? If you're in love, you don't. This is for those who are not yet at that stage, for whom we artificially and temporarily create the same "atmosphere" of uncertainty.

Again, without some doubt there is the feeling that "you will always be there." Then he no longer sees how great you are and loses appreciation for you. He begins to take you for granted and the passion dies. But you, in your relationship, can within a second reignite the passion and turn the relationship around by introducing an element of doubt. Passion is extinguished when there is no doubt because when there's no doubt you will be taken for granted. Just as in the previous example of going to the doctor: You never gave your hearing a second thought until you thought that it might not be there. When doubt is introduced into the equation it changes your perspective! I cannot stress this enough: *You will be taken for granted and not appreciated and the passion will go out of the relationship if all elements of doubt are removed.*

Unfortunately, when we are insecure about a relationship we harm it further by being clingier because we need reassurance. But in doing so you reinforce that you are forever his and remove in his mind any doubt that you might not always be there. And then passion is extinguished. It is a fact of human nature. But now that you understand you can use it to your advantage.

Remember that this and the other factors in this chapter are not ideas or tricks that work sometimes. These are laws that dictate human behavior. If you use them and operate within these parameters you can succeed at gaining complete leverage in any relationship. But finally, make sure that you don't make the mistake that most do when it comes to . . . *how you make them feel.*

 Power Point

Why can't I have an open, honest, and trusting relationship? You can, of course, but you have to wait until you are in *love* with *each other*—and here's why. The above three tactics are ego-based and are designed to get you to this point, but should be discontinued so that you can move on to a mature and lasting relationship. Briefly, love is the absence of ego or the "I." And once love takes root, the dynamics of the relationship change so that the *more* the person is available, and the more he does for you, the *more* you love him. As far as passion goes, you need only introduce some uncertainty should you feel that you are being taken for granted.

How You Make Them Feel

A person likes you based on how you make her feel about herself. This doesn't contradict the above. You should still maintain the above behavior—regarding your *attitude* and *availability*—but you do want to *treat the person well.* It is bad advice, though often given, that you don't want to build up someone's confidence, and be overly flattering and complimentary, because then she will "know that you like her" and back off. To a degree, we know this can be true, because when someone likes us, while we are flattered, we can find ourselves less interested in that person. This reaction comes courtesy of the rule that says, *We want what we can't have and want more of that which we have to work for.* Simply, if it falls in our laps we tend to have less appreciation for it.

But herein lies the crucial difference between being *attentive and kind* versus *telling her that she is your entire world and the only person for you.* (Because, as we talked about, this removes doubt and begins to erode the passion.) The former is more objective and has to do primarily with her. The latter involves your *relationship* and invokes the rule of scarcity. Notice the crucial difference between saying how much you like this person—which makes you lose leverage—and telling her that she is a likable and great person. Merely stating that somebody is terrific makes her feel great and makes you look great. It's a winning combination because it's only the confident person who tells another how wonderful and terrific she is. And we like confident and secure people! The distinction is often blurred and we end up trying to "play it cool" and not wanting to "show our hand." This accomplishes little and creates a cold and uncomfortable atmosphere. But lavishing this person with "objective" praise shows you in the best and most confident light and makes her feel great! Again, you want to let her know that you think she's great but *not* that she is your whole world and that you can't live without her.

The fastest way to lose leverage and to lose someone that you like is to do the opposite of the above. That means making yourself completely available, having no perspective, removing all doubt, and being uncomplimentary. Do this and you can be sure that you'll be back dating someone whom you don't like very much. And he'll stick around because you'll do all the right things.

Strategy Review

- *People want what they can't have and they want more of what they have to work for.* If you are easy to come, then you may be easy to let go.

- If you have an unbalanced life you will have a distorted view of the relationship. *Balance gives you perspective,* and perspective allows you to make better decisions in the relationship.

- When all doubt is removed, the person will take you for granted. *Introduce an element of uncertainty* to instantly reignite the passion.

- A person likes you based, in part, on how you make her feel about herself. *Make her feel good and she will feel good about you.*

- Read through the tactics in the following chapter to round out your overall strategy.

5

Get Anyone to See You as Pure Gold
#1 Rule of Selling Yourself in Every Area of Life

Here is one of the greatest truths in life: If you don't place a value on yourself, *somebody else will.* How do you get the best deal, the finest advantage, or the greatest edge in anything? Here's how: *Ask for the moon and settle for the stars.* In the previous chapter we talked about gaining leverage in relationships. But when you're in a relationship of any sort, you want to invoke the power of this law to give you the ultimate edge.

Almost everything in life is subjective. This means that there is no absolute truth and *opinions tend to become facts* in most new situations. All other information is then filtered through this new belief structure. If you want to give yourself, or anything for that matter, instant worth, you need to create the right image. In negotiations start off *very* high, even if it's a little unreasonable. This is important because *you* will have set the tone. (Bear in mind, you also don't want to be ridiculously high, because you want to be taken seriously.) Whenever you are dealing with someone or something of unknown value *the first one who places a value on it establishes its worth.* To be clear, when we speak of the value of a person, we mean the perceived value *to others*, not, of course, the individual's value as a human being. Therefore, *value* is an unknown quantity whose perception can be altered with the application of two specific psychological principles.

Whenever you're dealing with an intangible, establish its worth where you want it, and as long as there is no established value, you will not be seen as unreasonable. Let's say you're an amateur photographer—you take pictures as a hobby—and someone wants to hire you as a freelancer. How much do you charge? Well, some photographers charge as much as $10,000 a day. Are you in their league? Probably not, but if you charge $100 a day clearly you will not be perceived as one of the best. Will you be laughed at if you say your fee is $3,000 for the day? Not likely. Even if you think they can't afford to pay you that much, you're now negotiating from a very high starting point—one that *you've established*. In the end you can charge them much less and they will be elated because they are not getting a $500-a-day photographer. No, they're getting a $3,000-a-day photographer for a mere $500!

Let's take a look at how this law affects us in our daily life. Let's say that you're shopping and you notice a jacket that you think is reasonably priced at $69. You think, "Okay, not too bad." Then you realize it's *$690*. Suddenly your opinion of the jacket changes dramatically. You begin to realize that what you thought was *fair* quality is really *exquisite tailoring* and you "notice" every little detail and can now "see" how it could be so expensive. At $690 you might not buy it, but if it went on sale the next week for $129, you just might snatch it up. Why? Because of its *perceived* value.

Now there's one other factor other than price that helps to establish value. The other criterion that determines worth is how *available* something is. Simply, the *scarcer* something is, the greater the *value* people place on it. Gold, oil, and diamonds are much more valuable than water and air because they are not as plentiful. Even though water and air are indispensable to our survival, it's gold and precious jewels that we value. (Until, of course, you're without water for a day; then its scarcity makes it more valuable than a king's ransom.)

So how do you establish your "worth" in personal relationships? You can *make yourself more valuable by not being so available.* Sex? Give it freely initially, and little value is placed on it, and on you. This is as true for men as it is for women. At work . . . your time? If you're sitting by the water cooler all day, how do you think you'll be perceived by your boss and coworkers? Will you be judged as valuable or a dime a dozen?

Strategy Review

🖉 *Price* and *availability* are the most dominant psychological factors that determine the value of just about anything or any person. Manipulating these two factors will dramatically increase or decrease how valuable and worthy we think someone or something is.

6

How to Appear Calm, Confident, and in Control in Any Situation

These techniques are included in this section because as we talked about in the previous chapters, *confidence* and *likability* go together. We are attracted to, admire, and tend to like those whom we see as in control and secure in themselves. (There's nothing less attractive than a person who has a low opinion of himself.) And while this chapter won't give you self-esteem, the techniques can make you *appear* and actually *feel* more calm and confident. This will allow you to get into an *optimum state* in any situation or conversation.

The first influence to consider is the *physiological* aspect of anxiety. When we're nervous about giving a speech or meeting someone, for example, most of us don't eat or eat the wrong things. Anytime we eat foods high in sugar or refined carbohydrates our bodies produce adrenaline in an attempt to regulate our blood sugar levels. This is because these foods lower our blood sugar levels and the body produces *adrenaline* to compensate for the fluctuation. Adrenaline, which is the primary factor in the fight-or-flight response, is what *causes you* to become anxious and nervous. This is why people who eat a diet high in sugars and refined carbohydrates often seem nervous and high-strung. This is a psychological disorder that manifested from a poor diet.

Power Point

Recent studies show that those who suffer from obsessive-compulsive disorder (OCD), panic attacks, and anxiety attacks may find relief in a low-carbohydrate diet. By keeping blood sugar levels steady, anxiety-based symptoms can be greatly alleviated.

Have you ever noticed that after a large meal you feel fairly relaxed and calm? This is because your blood sugar level is stable and the body is not producing high levels of adrenaline to compensate for fluctuations. The ideal, though, is to eat *small nonrefined meals.* This will keep your blood sugar levels steady and your mind calm; you won't feel too sluggish to think clearly. (There are countless nutritional books that do a much better job on this subject than we can in this short space. Any health food store with a book section can give you full and complete information on nonrefined foods.)

Another fascinating aspect to consider is that the very things you do to *appear* calm and relaxed can actually *make you feel more calm and relaxed.* So by engaging in certain behaviors and avoiding others you can maintain a sense of calm and inner balance.

By changing your *physiology* you can actually change your *brain chemistry.* For example, studies show that when we *smile* we actually *put ourselves into a better mood.* It has long been thought that we smile when we feel happy—which is of course true. There is strong evidence, however, that *the act itself* can transform your emotional state and make you *feel happier.* Conversely, if you were to frown for a minute or so, you would probably feel worse. While our mood reflects our physical state so too does our physical self bring about a change in our mood. The most important, dominant factors that affect mood and our emotional state are:

✔ Smile. This is a universal sign that you are comfortable. And again, according to several studies, the *very act of smiling* calms you down and actually makes you feel more relaxed.

✔ Breathe! When we're nervous we tend to hold our breath. Breathe deeply and regularly. This will calm you down instantly and make it easier for you to think, react, and speak clearly and confidently.

 Power Point

Want to tell if anyone is nervous about anything? Look for these two signs. If they're not smiling and breathing regularly and deeply then they're not as calm as they would like you to believe! (You can tell if a person is *not* breathing regularly because you'll notice every so often he takes a very deep breath to get oxygen in very quickly.)

Research into this area also shows us something else remarkable. That is, our emotions are not just in our mind but actually in *every cell, in every organ,* and *in every muscle* of our body. If you want to ensure long-term emotional balance and calm, try yoga or some type of stretching routine. Our muscles retain our emotions. Haven't you ever wondered why you feel so good after you stretch out your body? The psychological tensions are released along with the physical stresses.

The central nervous system is made up of our brain and spinal cord. It is *impossible* to completely relax the mind unless you relax the spinal cord as well. Yoga helps to achieve this. Notice how high-strung and nervous people carry themselves. Their bodies are often tense and stiff. Working out the tensions in the physical body begins the process of releasing emotional stresses. In addition to smiling and deep breathing, try this for short-term and long-term success toward releasing negative emotions and relaxing yourself within minutes, *every time.*

Strategy Review

✎ Don't overlook the powerful *physiological* influence of blood sugar levels. Avoid engaging the fight-or-flight response by avoiding sugars and refined carbohydrates.

✎ *Smile!* Research shows that the very act of smiling actually makes you feel more relaxed and calm.

✐ *Breathe deeply.* When we're nervous we tend to hold our breath. Deep breathing *instantly relaxes* the central nervous system and literally calms your nerves.

✐ For long-term stress reduction practice yoga. The central nervous system is made up of the brain and spinal cord. It is impossible to feel completely relaxed mentally unless your *body* is at ease.

Section II

NEVER BE FOOLED, TRICKED, MANIPULATED, USED, LIED TO, OR TAKEN ADVANTAGE OF AGAIN

Are you tired of looking foolish and being taken advantage of? Let's face it, there are people in this world who are willing to say and do anything to get their way. Whether it's the car salesman, your date, a coworker, or your boss, knowing if they are out for their best interests or yours is invaluable. With these psychological tactics, you will be able to tell within minutes what somebody is really up to. If you're tired of getting the short end of the stick use these techniques and . . . never feel powerless again!

7

The Six-Star Test to See if Someone Is a True Friend

Does she really care about you? Is he loyal? Is he just pretending to like you? Sometimes it can be hard to sift out those who pretend to be our friends from real true friends. But you don't have to waste time in dead-end or selfish relationships anymore. With these psychological secrets you'll never have to worry whether he's got your best interests at heart—or his own! You'll know for sure, every time. This might be a good place to remind you that friendship is the foundation for *any relationship*. If you are with someone who fails this test, the relationship may not be a very sound one.

THE SIX-STAR TEST TO SEE IF SHE'S A TRUE FRIEND

◆ *Interest*
One important criterion that defines a friend is *how interested the person is in your life.* Tell her about something significant that is going on in your life and see if she calls to follow up and find out what happened. If she doesn't, then call her and see if she mentions it. Finally, if she doesn't bring it up, hint about it and see if she even remembers the conversation you had about it previously.

◆ *Loyalty*
Tell a secret about a mutual friend and see if it gets back to him or her. *True friends know the value of trust in a relationship.* Just make sure that you get the permission of your friend to tell her secret to this other person.

◆ *Pride*

Anyone can tell you to cheer up. It makes *them* feel good. But see who pats you on the back for a good job. Those who are not driven by jealousy and envy will do just that. Your true friends are *proud of your accomplishments,* not jealous of your successes. See if a friend comes to you when you get good news, not just bad news. There are lots of people who are willing to "cheer us up" when things aren't going well. But it's more difficult to find someone who will congratulate us when things are going well.

◆ *Honesty*

A true friend is someone who tells you the things that you don't want to hear. She is willing to have you be upset with her if it will help you. Does she tell you things that are for your benefit even though she knows that it might make you upset with her?

◆ *Respect*

Tell her that there is something exciting—something that is good—going on in your life but you absolutely prefer not to talk about it right now and see if she presses you on it. There's a difference between *curiosity* and *concern.* If she "must know" then she's just interested in the gossip and not in you. A good friend will respect your wishes and give you your space—for now. She may bring it up from time to time, because she's interested, but she won't constantly and immediately press you on it if you *make it clear* that you choose not to discuss it now. The reason you use a positive instead of a negative "mystery" is because if a good friend feels that something is wrong or that you are not well, she will *insist* on knowing *now* because *she is concerned.* You don't want to "test" her this way, however, because you wouldn't want to put your friend through this.

◆ *Sacrifice*

Is she willing to give up something if it means making you happy? Will she sacrifice her own pleasure for your happiness? Who decides what you do? Is the word *compromise* in her vocabulary? And when the chips are down and it's you against them, most people scramble to protect their own interests. Notice if she is the one who has ideas or a plan to help both of you to "escape unscathed" or whether she just looks to save herself and protect her own interests.

Strategy Review

✎ If she passes four or more of the six tests, you've probably got a good friend whom you can count on. If she scores three or less, you might want to review your friendship or speak to her about it. Of course, when we have a lot going on in our own lives we can become inadvertently distracted and unintentionally insensitive. So it's best to gauge the relationship using these six factors over a period of time and not just in a twenty-four-hour period.

8

Does His Story Check Out?

How to Spot a False Alibi by Asking a Single Question

Have you ever wanted to hook somebody up to a lie detector test to see if he was telling you the truth? Well, now with this technique you can *instantly* find out if his story checks out or if his alibi is nothing but a pack of lies. The technique used here is called *conundrum*. It works by introducing a piece of evidence and watching how your "suspect" handles it. You'll see that you can tell if anyone is lying by asking one question, and you can use this technique in *any situation* when you want to check on someone's alibi.

Let's say a woman suspected that her husband was not at the movies with his friends, as he said, but out with his secretary for a late night rendezvous. Simply asking him if he really did go to the movies would only prompt him to answer *yes*. This is because if he was there he would say *yes* and if he wasn't there he would likely stick to his story and say *yes*. And she wouldn't know whether or not to believe him. With this psychological technique *she introduces a made-up "fact"* and then sees how he handles it.

For instance she might say, "Oh, I heard that the traffic was all backed up because of a car accident right outside the theater." Now all she has to do is sit back and watch how he responds.

This is because her husband is faced with an obvious conundrum. If he wasn't at the movies, he doesn't know whether to acknowledge that there was an accident because there might not have been one. And if he says that there wasn't much traffic and there was, then she'll also know he wasn't really at the movies. But regardless of his answer, he will do the one thing that *every liar does* when confronted with *conundrum*: He will *hesitate—deciding* how to answer.

Remember, had he been at the theater he would have instantly said, "There was no traffic. What are you talking about?" But the liar isn't sure because *he wasn't there,* and so he will hesitate in his answer and in doing so *give himself away.* On top of that, he will likely answer wrongly by *agreeing to what you say,* because he doesn't know that you're making up the accident.

 Power Point

It's all in the details. The more *detailed* he is the more you can believe in what he's saying. Made-up stories often have huge gaps and are vague and abstract. How specific is his story?

Strategy Review

To use *conundrum,* simply introduce a piece of evidence and see how he handles it. Just make sure that he would have *direct knowledge* of what you're talking about if in fact his story is true. Make sure that this "evidence" is something that's *plausible* but *not true,* then sit back and see whether he's fast with the correct response. If he *hesitates, changes the subject,* and/or gives the *wrong answer* to your question, then you're *not* getting the truth.

9

How to Tell if Someone Is Trying to Manipulate You

The Seven Deadly Tricks to Watch Out For

From the bedroom to the boardroom learn how to see clearly and easily evaluate information without being swayed by those with selfish interests and unkind intentions. The manipulator's bag of tricks is stocked with *seven* deadly tactics that can have you jumping through hoops. The good news is that by knowing what they are, you can watch out for them, and . . . never be manipulated again!

These powerful manipulators are: *guilt, intimidation, appeal to ego, fear, curiosity, our desire to be liked,* and *love.* Anyone who uses any of these is attempting to move you from logic to emotion—to a playing field that's not so level. He knows that he can't win on the facts so he will try to manipulate your emotions with any one or a combination of the tactics below.

- Guilt: "How can you even say that? I'm hurt that you wouldn't trust me. I just don't know who you are anymore."
- Intimidation: "What's the matter, can't you make a decision? Don't you have enough confidence in yourself to do this?"
- Appeal to Ego: "I can see that you're a smart person. I wouldn't try to put anything past you. How could I? You'd be on to me in a second."
- Fear: "You know, you might just lose this whole thing. I sure hope you know what you're doing. I'm telling you that you won't get a better deal anywhere else. This is your last shot at making things work out; why do you want to risk losing out on being happy?"

- Curiosity: "Look, you only live once. Try it. You can always go back to how things were before. It might be fun, exciting—a real adventure. You'll never know unless you try and you may regret never even seeing what happens."

- Our Desire to Be Liked: "I thought you were a real player. So did everybody else. This is going to be a real disappointment if you don't come through for us. Come on, nobody likes it when a person backs out . . . this can be your chance to prove what you're made of."

- Love: "If you loved me you wouldn't question me. Of course I have only your best interests at heart. I wouldn't lie to you. You know that deep down inside, don't you? We can have a wonderful relationship if only you'd let yourself go and experience the wonders that the future will deliver to us."

Strategy Review

Look and listen objectively—not only to the words but also to the message. These abusive maneuvers interfere with your ability to digest the facts. When these emotions creep into your thinking, temporarily suspend your feelings and look at the *messenger* as well as the *message*. If you hear anything that sounds like these manipulators, *stop* and *reevaluate* the situation. *Don't act quickly and emotionally.* Wait and objectively gather the facts so you don't become a hand puppet for the malevolent.

10

How to Tell if a Person's Bluffing in Any Situation

How would you like to know if the guy sitting across the poker table from you really has a full house or just a pair of deuces? Or if your top executive is serious about quitting if he doesn't get a raise? There is a way to tell just about anytime, in any situation, if someone is bluffing because no matter what the situation *all bluffs have one thing in common.*

To understand how this works let's define what a bluff really is. A bluff occurs when a person is really against something *but pretends* to be for it. Or when he is for something and pretends to be against it. Consequently, when a person bluffs he usually tries to appear as if he doesn't care when he really does, and he pretends to be concerned when he really isn't.

In any case, *he is trying to create a false impression* intended to disguise his true belief. Therein lies the key: People who bluff generally *overcompensate,* in either direction, and if you look for it, it's glaringly obvious.

You can uncover a bluff instantly by noticing how someone *tries to appear.* A card player bets heavily and raises the pot. Does he have the cards or just guts? When bluffing—in this case, in a poker hand—he wants to show that he's not timid. So he puts in his money fast. But if he did have a good hand, what might he do? That's right, deliberate a bit, putting it in slowly to show that he isn't really sure about his hand. When people bluff at anything, in poker or in the real world, *they manipulate how* confident *they appear.* This means that they try to create the opposite impression of how they truly feel.

Again, while bluffing, and in trying to *appear confident,* he bets quickly. And when he has a good hand he will actually wait a moment or two to *pretend* that he's thinking about what to do. This goes for all situations. If he reacts too quickly and assuredly then he is trying to *show* that he is confident, when in many cases he really isn't.

Let's take another example. A partner in a law firm says he's going to leave unless he is allowed to take on a certain case. Is it a hollow threat or the real McCoy? If it was genuine, he would likely *not* make a point of trying to convey his confidence. However, an air of over-confidence will be easily observed if he is bluffing. This is, of course, because we have to assume that if he's at the firm then he wants to be there. And that he will only be "forced" to leave if he doesn't get what he's asking for. So logic dictates that he would *rather stay and get the case than not get it and leave.* Therefore, if he appears overly com-mitted to the idea of leaving if he doesn't get the case, then he's bluff-ing—because we know that he really doesn't want to leave, but is trying to create that impression.

If he is sincere in his stance that he will leave if he doesn't get his way, then he will appear almost *reluctant* and not overly confident in his stance because he's not pleased that it has come down to this. He's more solemn because he knows that he will have to leave if it comes down to it. But if he was bluffing, it won't come down to any-thing, because he's not leaving! The attitudes of both are completely different and make it clear whether it's a bluff or the real thing.

To understand the psychology behind this, we need only look at how people handle themselves in general. A person who has high self-esteem and confidence in himself is *not* the one going around showing the world how great he is. It's *the insecure person* who puts on airs of confidence, almost arrogance, to compensate for how he really feels about himself. He is, in fact, trying to convey a "false self." And as we've just illustrated, this is identical and true for specific sit-uations as well.

In a negotiation the person who keeps saying things such as, "I'm gonna walk; you have to do right by me; I'm not settling on this one: you're going to lose me," is not going anywhere . . . he's bluffing. Confidence in one's position usually speaks for itself. Just as a per-son's confidence *in himself* speaks for itself. It's the insecure who has to *tell you* how confident he is because that's the only way that we're going to find out. If, however, you hear something similar to the fol-lowing phrases in a negotiation, they likely reflect a person who is sincere, and who is not bluffing: "I'm sorry that you feel that way; no hard feelings; I don't think so, but let me give it some thought." Remember that the confident person—the one who is not bluffing—isn't interested in how he's coming across. He's unconcerned with his image, unlike his bluffing counterpart, who is consumed by others' perceptions of him.

Strategy Review

    ✐ Uncover a bluff instantly by noticing how the person *tries* to appear. A person who is bluffing will always *overcompensate* to create the illusion that he is 100 percent behind his convictions.

11

How to See Through People

In Two Minutes Get Anyone to Reveal What They're Really Up To

If you're tired of being deceived and taken advantage of, this psychological technique will allow you to actually look into a person's mind to find out if he's hiding anything.

The tactic, which I first introduced in my book *Never Be Lied to Again,* virtually guarantees that you can find out if he's got something to hide, within minutes. It's called *similar scenario* and it works like a Rorschach test or what is commonly referred to as an inkblot test. The Rorschach test consists of abstract bilaterally symmetrical inkblots. The theory behind the test is that a person's interpretation of the shapes will reveal his or her unconscious attitudes and thoughts. With *similar scenario* we use the same theory but employ it in an entirely new way—*verbally.*

What you want to do is to ask a question that does not *accuse* the person of anything but rather *alludes* to it. Then by simply gauging his response you'll be able to find out if he's got something to hide.

For instance let's say that a woman suspects her husband of having an affair with his secretary. Casually, maybe over dinner, she would say, "Gee, you know what, honey? My boss, Jim, I think he may be having an affair with *his* secretary." Now she simply observes his reaction. If he *asks questions and becomes interested in the conversation* she can be reasonably sure that he's *not* doing the same thing. But if he becomes very uncomfortable and looks to change the subject, then it's likely *he's engaged in a similar behavior.* And she will notice this immediate shift in his demeanor and attitude.

 **Power Point**

Typically, when faced with this situation we confront the person, which of course puts him on the defensive. If it turns out that we're wrong, there's a good chance that we may appear as paranoid or jealous and the relationship may suffer. With this technique we're able to bring up a particular subject and find out if he's *comfortable* or *concerned* with the topic, and all without making a single accusation.

Let's look at another example. You think one of your salespeople is stealing office supplies. Asking outright, "Have you been stealing from the company?" is going to put her on the defensive immediately, making it nearly impossible to get to the truth. If she isn't guilty she'll tell you that she hasn't been stealing. And if she is, she'll likely lie and say she's isn't. So instead you simply say, "Jill, I'm wondering if you could help me with something. It's come to my attention that someone in the sales department has been taking home office supplies for personal use. Any idea on how we can put a stop to this?"

Again, if she's innocent of the charges she's likely to offer her advice and be pleased that you sought out her opinion. But if she's guilty you'll notice her becoming very *uncomfortable* and she will probably assure you that *she would never do anything like that.* There's no reason for her to bring herself into the picture unless, of course, she's the one who feels guilty.

Do you see how effective this technique is? Let's take one more example where a hospital administrator suspects that a doctor is drinking while on duty. She might say, "Dr. Marcus, I'd like to get your advice on something. A colleague of mine at another hospital has a problem with one of her doctors. She feels that he may be drinking while on call. Do you have any suggestions on how she can best approach this doctor?"

Again, if he's guilty of the same behavior he'll become very uncomfortable. If he's not drinking on duty, then he will be pleased that you sought his advice and willingly and happily offer it. So whenever you're wondering what somebody's up to, use a *similar scenario* and find out for sure.

Strategy Review

✎ Give him the instant psychological test. Ask a question that does not *accuse* the person of anything but rather *alludes* to it. Then simply gauge his response and you'll learn right away if he's hiding anything.

12

Get Anyone to Say What He's Really Thinking

Ever wish you could peer into someone's mind to find out what he really thinks about you, your idea, your project, or your date? *Now you can* with the ultimate mind-reading technique that actually uses a combination of several psychological principles. When you think someone isn't telling you the truth this sure-fire technique is an excellent method for revealing a person's *true feelings* in any situation.

Getting a truthful *opinion* from someone can be hard because you can't outright call him a liar, arguing that he doesn't really believe what he is saying. For this technique to work, you just have to get the person to commit to *liking* the idea/person, etc. (If he doesn't like it, then you don't have to worry about trying to get the truth because you're already getting it.)

Once she says that she likes it, *don't argue or press her on it.* This is exactly where most people mess up. They'll say something like, "Are you sure you like it? Do you really?" The other person is not now going to say, "Well, now that I think of it . . ." She's going to become more absolute in her approval and you may not be getting to what she really thinks.

With this technique, you'll see that the words you use in your response indicate that you *agree* and that there is room for improvement. She feels comfortable offering criticism because she feels that you *expect* her to do so. The two main psychological tactics at work here are *consistency* (human beings have a need for continuity with their thinking) and *expectancy* (people often do what is expected of them). Both of these concepts are covered more extensively in other sections throughout this book.

Example I

You're not sure if your coworker really likes your idea for a new marketing campaign, even though she says that she does.

Q: Do you *like* the concept for my new idea?

A: Sure. It's very original.

Q: Well, what would it take for you to *love* the idea?

Example II

You want to know if your son is looking forward to going to camp this summer.

Q: Are you *excited* about camp next month?

A: Yeah. It'll be fun.

Q: What would it take for you to be *really excited* about going?

Example III

Q: Do you *like* my new deck?

A: Sure, it looks fine.

Q: How do you think I can make it even better?

As you can see, all these people feel comfortable answering honestly because your questions to them make it obvious that *you know that everything's not perfect.* By *not* pressing the point of their *liking* it, their answer naturally unfolds as an extension of what they've already said, and the truth—what they're really thinking—merely "pops" out.

 Power Point

Are you trying to find out what she thinks, but she doesn't want to speak ill of someone else or his work? No problem. Instead of saying, "What didn't you like about it?" or "How did she screw up?" ask instead, "How would you have done it?" or "What would you have done differently?" This phrasing takes the focus off what the other person did wrong, and instead asks what this person would have done to make it better. But as you see you get the identical information.

Strategy Review

✐ Just get her to commit to *liking* the idea, person, or object. Then simply ask her how she thinks that it can be improved upon.

TAKE CONTROL OF ANY SITUATION AND GET ANYONE TO DO ANYTHING

Succeeding in life is usually a matter of influencing the attitudes, beliefs, and thoughts of other people. This is not success through manipulation, but rather success through the application of specific psychological strategies. There's a big difference. This book operates under the premise that most people are good, decent, and honest. (Of course, there are people who are not so great and this book will protect you from them as well so you won't be manipulated and taken advantage of.) But as you know from your own life, often our fears and hang-ups get in the way of our doing what's right for ourselves and for others. Most people *want to help*; it makes them *feel good* to do for others. So rather than force people to bend to your will, this section shows you how to naturally bring out the pure and good desire and intentions of others to help you and to work with you.

You can easily direct the behavior and thoughts of other people by *your* words and *your* actions. *By changing the things that you do and say to others you'll change their attitudes and behavior toward you.* It's really that simple. People do not operate in a vacuum but instead they think and behave in response to their world. *Change their world and you change their responses.*

Depending on the situation, you can use whichever strategies best apply. If you simply want someone to help you with something, then go to Chapter 17, Get Anyone to Do a Favor for You. If, however, you need to first change a person's mind about something, then you should go to Chapter 16, How to Get a Stubborn Person to Change His Mind About Anything. These tactics are designed to work alone and as part of an overall strategy that uses tactics from the various chapters and sections.

13

Get Anyone to Take Immediate Action in Any Situation

You are about to see that by following a simple formula that uses *six different psychological tactics,* you can motivate anyone to take action anytime. This powerful strategy as outlined below virtually guarantees cooperation from anyone in just about any situation.

1. LIMIT OPTIONS

The first thing you want to do is *narrow someone's options before you present them* to him. Conventional wisdom suggests that with more options he is sure to find something that he likes and that this will *motivate* him to take action. The opposite is true! If what you want him to do has numerous alternatives he will be less likely to choose any of them. Nobody enjoys being wrong and we don't like to second-guess ourselves. Fewer choices mean that he will make a decision *faster* and be less likely to dwell on it afterward.

There is a well-known furniture chain that holds on to every customer order for seventy-two hours before putting it through to the home office. Why? Because it found that over 60 percent of people, within three days of a major purchase, will come back to change their mind about the color, a fabric, or the design. With too many choices most people freeze and take forever to decide, and once they do make a decision, their brain often churns with *Did I make the right choice?* Unless you're in a retail situation where competition mandates selection, offer no more than three options, with two being ideal. No choices can lead to a person's feeling his freedom is restricted and cause him to back off. Any option, even one, gives him a sense of empowerment and you want him to *believe* that he's in control.

2. Give a Deadline

Giving a deadline for action fulfills three separate and very important psychological motivations for fostering action.

- A task will expand or contract depending upon how much time you allow for it. The world operates on deadlines and expiration dates because if there is no immediate need to move forward most people will not. It is human nature to wait until conditions become more *favorable,* or until we have *more information,* or until we are in a *better mood* before taking an action. It's important to give a clear-cut deadline and let the person know that the action must be taken *now* because he may not have a chance to act later.

- This also invokes another psychological motivation in that we don't like our freedom to be restricted. Whenever we are told that we *cannot* have or do something we end up *desiring it more.* So by letting an individual know that he may not get the opportunity to act in the future, you create a larger incentive toward moving now. There is another well-known though less scrupulous retail store that puts "sold" tags on items that it *wants to get rid of.* They do it for this very reason. When we see a "sold" tag on something we are unconsciously driven to desire it more. Then when we find out that another "just like it" may be for sale we jump on the opportunity to purchase it.

- Consistent with this law are numerous studies that show that human beings respond to that which is scarce and becoming scarcer. I'm sure you find this to be true in your own life. When something is the latest or hottest and everyone wants one, it becomes that much more desirable. And when the window of opportunity to act *continues to shrink,* we are driven to desire it *that much more.* We place value on that which is scarce. Diamonds, gold, and oil are not essential to our well-being yet they are highly valued—but only because of the *perception that they are scarce.* Think about it. Platinum is worth more than gold and gold more than silver and silver more than copper. *All because of how much of it is available to us.*

3. USE THE LAW OF INERTIA

Sir Isaac Newton first informed us that objects in motion tend to stay in motion, and objects at rest tend to stay at rest. He might well have added that *people* in motion tend to stay in motion and people at rest tend to stay at rest. If you are able to get the person moving in the right direction, either physically or mentally—starting with something easy and/or fun—he will likely continue to follow through. Why is this so?

Human beings have a strong need for consistency with their actions. Several studies in this area clearly illustrate how effective this psychological factor can be when applied to motivating a person. They show us that when someone is presented with a small request and subsequently does it, *he is infinitely more likely to agree to a larger request*—the thing that we wanted him to do in the first place—what we *really* wanted him to do. However, if he is not first presented with, and subsequently doesn't complete, the smaller request, then he has no unconscious motivation for consistency.

Called the "foot-in-the-door technique," the following study demonstrates the tendency for people who have first agreed to a small request to comply later with a larger request. Freedman and Fraser (1966) asked home owners if they would let them place a huge DRIVE CAREFULLY sign in their front yards. *Only 17 percent gave permission.* Other residents, however, were first approached with a smaller request. They were asked to put up a three-inch BE A SAFE DRIVER window sign. Nearly all immediately agreed. When approached a few weeks later the home owners were asked to place the gigantic sign on their front lawn. This same group overwhelmingly agreed—*76 percent consented*—to having the unsightly sign in their front yards.

When we take a small step in one direction we are *driven to maintain a sense of consistency* by agreeing to larger requests. Simply, those who had agreed to the smaller request had reshaped their self-concept to include the definition that *they were serious about driver safety*. Therefore, agreeing to the larger request was just doing something for a cause that they *already* and *firmly* "believed" in. Effective fund-raisers know the number-one rule for raising money. The easiest person to get a donation from is someone who has given money before.

 Power Point

Music has an impact on the speed of our actions. Consider the study done by Milliman (1982), which showed that slow-paced music played in grocery stores increases sales because shoppers walk more slowly down the aisles. The flip side of this is also true. Fast-paced music furnishes an unconscious motivation for acting quickly. Roballey et al. (1985) found that if fast music is played while people eat, they *respond with more bites per minute*. If possible, have fast-tempo music playing in the background to increase the feeling and urgency for taking action. To increase the benefits of this law try *speaking faster*. You will notice that if you ask someone a question slowly, he will respond the same way, and vice versa. Others will be guided by your sense of urgency and speaking fast increases this feeling of necessity.

---

4. EXPECTATION

The law of expectation states that people will do what you expect them to do. *Speak and act directly, clearly, and confidently.* Also, take the appropriate corresponding physical action. Whether it's moving toward the door, picking up a pen, or dialing the phone, people will respond to your assuredness and act accordingly. In other words, you can use more than just *words*—use your *actions* as well—to spark action. If, for example, you want someone to follow you—literally—begin walking without looking back "to make sure he's coming." Your words and actions must convey *confidence* and *expectation* that the person will comply.

5. PROCESSING INFORMATION

It is crucial to this process to know how people process information. The good news is that we all do it in the same way. In my book *Never Be Lied to Again* I talked about this concept and how it gives us a dramatic insight into human behavior. Remember above when we spoke about starting with something easy and simple to enact the law of inertia? Let's take a look at another application of this process. When it comes to doing something that we like, we do what's called *single-tasking*. When we think about things we don't want to do, we do what's called *multitasking*. What does this all mean? Well, if you have to pay your bills but never feel like doing it, what are the thought processes you might go through? You think, I've got to get all of the bills together and organize them into different piles; get out my checkbook, stamps, and envelopes; address each letter; write out the check; balance the checkbook; and so on. When it comes to doing something you enjoy doing, you internalize the steps in larger groups. For example, if you enjoy cooking, the steps might be, go to the store and come home and make dinner.

If you hated to cook, everything from waiting on line at the supermarket to cleaning the dishes afterward would enter into the equation. Fine, but what's the practical use of this? Well, if you want someone to take immediate action, you're going to show him that it's *simple* and *easy*. If you want to *discourage* a behavior, you need only stretch out the number of steps into a long, boring, and arduous process. It's the same event, but depending upon how it's internalized, you'll generate a completely different attitude toward it.

6. ADDITIONAL INCENTIVE

But wait . . . that's not all! How many times have you heard this familiar phrase at the end of a commercial or late night infomercial? The "add-on" is a highly effective tool for generating action whether on TV, in person, or on the phone. *So use it.* It's estimated that the use of this technique increases the response rate from these programs by as much as 35 *percent.* It gives the person an extra benefit for acting, and the most fascinating thing is that it almost doesn't matter what it is. Once you've presented your request by employing the tactics above, use an "add-on." It can be *any small additional benefit* that the person gets for taking action *now* (i.e., "We can get ice cream"; "I'll have a loaner car for you"; "We'll go to dinner afterward," etc.). You'll be amazed at how efficient this psychological tool can be.

 ## Power Point

The language that you use can also invoke the law of inertia. Seemingly innocuous words such as: *as, while,* and *during* are such powerful motivators that they are often used in hypnosis. Remember that when a person is already in motion—either in thought or physically—it's easier for him to continue. For example if you want compliance, you're better off saying something such as, "*While* we're out let's go by Jim's house, okay?" instead of, "When we go out, do you want to stop in and see Jim?" Do you see how easily the first sentence flows with the idea of seeing Jim?

Strategy Review

✎ Narrow a person's options to avoid extensive deliberation. Fewer choices mean that he will make a decision *faster* and be less likely to dwell on it afterward.

✎ Give a deadline for taking action. A deadline restricts freedom and increases our desire to gain what is rare and becoming scarcer. This greatly motivates us to move forward and to take immediate action.

✎ Engage the law of consistency by first having an individual commit to a smaller request. When we take a small step in one direction we are *driven to maintain a sense of consistency* by agreeing to larger requests.

✎ Use *your words* and *your actions* to engage the law of expectation.

✎ Maximize the law of inertia by reducing what you want a person to do to simple, easy-to-follow steps to get him to begin moving in the right direction.

✎ Offer any *small additional benefit* for taking action *now*. This will significantly increase your chances of gaining compliance.

✎ Keep in mind that the *number-one* psychological rule that determines if someone will do something for you or even with you is that she must, to some extent, *like you* and, preferably, *trust you*. So glance at Chapter 1, Get Anyone to Like You . . . Every Time, in order to round out your psychological strategy for this section.

14

Get Anyone to *Take* Your Advice

You've got a great idea but nobody is listening to you! This can be extremely frustrating but by following a specific psychological strategy you can virtually ensure that anyone will listen to what you have to say. The three main factors of influence here are (1) emotions, (2) strategy, and (3) consequences.

It's been clearly established, through numerous studies, that you need to *appeal to a person's emotions* in your attempt to persuade. No matter how rational and logical your argument is, if you do not arouse emotions you will have great difficulty influencing him.

Ninety percent of the decisions we make are based on emotion. We then use *logic* to *justify* our actions. If you appeal to someone on a strictly logical basis, you will have little chance of persuading him. You need to translate the facts into an emotion-based statement— and give *clear* and *specific benefits* that appeal to the person's *emotions.*

Studies show that in addition to arousing strong emotions you will be especially effective when you offer a *specific game plan* with a *clear-cut course of action* for proceeding. When we are passionately motivated to take action and move forward, it is essential that we *understand* the *direction* and the *method* for proceeding. It makes us feel *comfortable* and *secure* knowing that the path is clearly lit and laid out. When you want someone to listen to your advice, provide more than just the desired destination; also give her a map for getting there.

It has been shown that if you add to this how your idea will *prevent* negative or unpleasant consequences you will be infinitely more successful in your attempt to persuade (Leventhal, Singer, and Jones, 1965). A well-known sweepstakes company used to have a slogan that said: *You can be a winner.* It did very well with this for a long time. But then, I'm sure after consulting a psychologist or two, its slogan changed to *You may* already *be a winner.* This greatly increased their success. Why? Because now the person receiving this envelope became fearful that he might *lose* something that he already had. Throw out an envelope that contains untold riches? No way! This was different than *gaining something new,* as the old slogan implied. Now he risked *losing* something. This is a much more powerful motivator. Therefore, focus on what he will be saving himself from (i.e., the heartache, money, energy, etc.) rather than what he has to *gain* from listening to you.

Four other psychological factors to consider

- ➤ People tend to respond more favorably to solutions if they believe the plan of action came from them. Try to remind someone that it was he who first had the idea or put you in the right direction, etc.
- ➤ Let him know too that this new way of thinking is really consistent with *who he is.* Remind him of other things he's done that are consistent with this current belief or action. You may recall from a previous chapter that *all* human beings have an inherent need for order and consistency. If he views this as a continuation of his thinking and not a departure from it, you'll increase your chances of getting compliance.
- ➤ Nobody wants to hear advice from a "know-it-all." One of the very best ways of offering advice is to let the person know that you don't believe you have all the answers. You'll be perceived as infinitely more credible and sincere. A great way to phrase your advice is, "There are things I think I know, and there are things I know I know. And this is something that I know I know."
- ➤ Above all, remember enthusiasm is contagious. The more excited and passionate you are about what you're saying the more excited he will become about it.

Follow this strategy for sure-fire success, but before you do, let's take a look at one of the biggest mistakes that people make when giving advice. This aspect of human nature is responsible for more "stubborn" thinking than anything else. Research in human behavior shows us that *when we feel our freedom is being restricted or limited we tend to move farther toward what is being limited.*

The name given to this is called *reactance* and it occurs when we feel that someone is trying to limit our freedom. And it can be so powerful that Rhodewalt and Davison (1983) found that people may do the *opposite* of what you are asking—just because of reactance.

In situations that are likely to generate reactance you will meet with great resistance if you promote a *hard sell.* No one will listen with an open mind to what you have to say, if he feels he's being forced into it. And in fact, that makes sense. Why listen if you feel that your own wishes aren't being considered? Therefore, the best approach is to let the person know ahead of time that he has the final say on what he ultimately does. Then lay out the facts, presenting both sides—the pros and the cons (you'll see in another chapter why this is necessary) and follow the rest of the tactics in this section.

Strategy Review

- Ninety percent of the decisions we make are based on emotion. We then use *logic* to *justify* our actions. *You must arouse emotions in your attempt to persuade.*
- Offer a *specific game plan* with a *clear-cut course of action* for proceeding.
- Add to this how your idea will *prevent* negative or unpleasant consequences. This is more effective than explaining what someone will *gain* by listening to you.
- If true, remind him how he is in some way the one who first gave you the idea.
- Let him know too that this new way of thinking is really consistent with *who he is.* Relate the things he's done that are consistent with this current belief or action.

🖉 Don't come across as a "know-it-all" and you'll be perceived as more credible and sincere in this situation.

🖉 Remember that *enthusiasm is contagious*. If you're not excited about the idea, he will not be excited about it either.

15

Get Anyone to Follow Through on a Commitment to You

"But you promised!" If you're tired of saying this, the following strategy will help to ensure that you'll be able to get any person to follow through on *anything* that he's promised to you.

The most effective psychological tool for getting someone to follow through is to let him know that *you believe* that he is the *type of person* who *does follow through.* Using phrases such as "You're the kind of person who . . ."; "You've always impressed me with your ability to . . ."; or "I've always liked the fact that you . . ." invokes the powerful psychological law of internal consistency.

These phrases make the person feel compelled to follow through because you involve the ego and create a sense of desired consistency. People have an inherent need to perform in a manner consistent with *how they see themselves* and with how they think others perceive them. That's why one of the biggest mistakes people make is saying things like, "Come on, please do it"; "I just knew this was going to be a problem"; "I just knew you weren't going to do this"; or "I don't know why I bothered to count on you." This does not generate any psychological motivation to prove you wrong. These comments address someone's *actions* not her *identity* and *force her ego to come up with reasons to* justify *her behavior, not to change it*!

For example, let's say you've asked someone to work on some files for you over the next two weeks. Don't say, "How are they coming?" or "Shouldn't you have started by now?" This only provides an opportunity for either an excuse or a chance for her to back out. Instead say, "You know, Sally, I appreciate your helping me with those files. I respect the fact that you're the kind of person who not only offers to help but follows through until she gets the job done." With these words you've wrapped this person's self-concept into a single cause. How you see her is woven into her behavior toward this project. You can be sure she will comply and continue working on it so that your image of her is not tarnished. This makes it nearly impossible for her to say, "I'm too busy or I don't feel like doing it." Because not only would she risk your questioning who she is but this would leave her wondering as well. Simply, she fancies seeing herself as someone who "follows through on things . . . and can be counted on," etc. If she abandons this project, then she has to ask herself, "What kind of person am I?" This is something very few people are willing or able to do.

Another version of this tactic—which can also be used in conjunction with the first one—is to invoke a *generic value identity*. For instance, you can incorporate themes such as friendship, commitment to work, a sense of decency—all qualities that most people aspire to identify with. A question like, "Isn't it amazing how some people don't know the definition of the word *friendship*?" is so powerful. With this one statement you bring her value system—what is important to her—into the task. Now this is not an isolated job, but something that actually *defines your friendship*. She's risking more than just annoying you by bailing out; she's risking the relationship. Instead of this just being an isolated project, you're able to bring your entire friendship and the power that it has into this one task.

These psychology-laden phrases will help keep her moving along, but when you want someone to follow through, it's crucial to lay the groundwork *when you first ask for the favor*. Take a look at the following study and then we'll discuss it.

Angela Lipsitz and others (1989) report that ending *blood-drive reminder calls* with, "We'll count on seeing you then, okay?" and then pausing for response increased the show-up rate from 62 *to 81 percent*. Just this one phrase increased the rate by about 20 percent. When you initially ask for the favor, make sure that you give a quick *verbal confirmation*. This *dramatically increases the level of internal consistency* as you solidify your chances of getting someone to follow through.

Power Point

Keep in mind that the *act of volunteering* makes it more likely that a person will follow through. If a certain task was thrust upon someone, you're going to risk an internal justification—where the thinking might be, "If I don't follow through, he'll be mad. I will feel guilty or suffer some form of retribution." This can hinder his enthusiasm for completing the task if he's able to resolve this internal conflict. In other words, he's not doing it because he's a great guy who follows through, but rather because *he has to.* To override this thinking (when you think it may be a problem), you just need to include the phrase, "I know you could have gotten out of it if you wanted to."

This is because when we volunteer, cognitive dissonance is reduced with the continuing thought that "I must really want to be doing this." The only other rationale is, "I'm an idiot and I never should have agreed to this." Most people's psyches are more comfortable with the first rationalization. This is why we often see people doing things that seem completely absurd or out of character for them.

But wait, there's more! When you initially ask a person for the favor, follow this *five-phase process* to *solidify* his *intent* to help.

You tell a friend, for example, that you're having problems with your computer and he cheerfully offers to try to come by next Saturday. Now, he just might be saying this to be nice or because he actually intends to try to come by. But you really need his help, and to make sure you get it, you want to move him *internally* and turn a casual offer into a firm commitment. You'll see that by applying a specific psychological sequence, you can take a vague offer and turn it into a *specific, firm commitment.*

Five-Step Process

1. Get him to say it: When you say it, it's one thing, but when he says it, it takes his commitment to a whole new level. *You want him to say the words.* Therefore, you say, "Do you really mean

that?" or "Are you serious?" He will most likely respond with, "Yes, I'll help you on Saturday."

2. Get a specific time frame: You want him to commit to a time in which he will help you and/or to a time frame of how long it will take for him to complete his task. In this example, you would say, "Great, what time?" and "Any idea of how long it might take?"

3. Develop a sense of obligation: It's important to let him know that because of his help, you are going to in some way *alter* what you were going to do. Viewing his help as a plus is only part of it. He needs, too, to see that the *withdrawal* of his offer will cause a disturbance. If he reneges and there are no repercussions, then he will see that things are no worse off for you than before he offered. In this case, you might let him know that you are canceling other appointments and moving your schedule around to accommodate him.

4. A sense of conscience: You want to relay that you are now *dependent* upon him for his help. Now is the time where you let him know how *important* his help really is. Mention any consequences that you might suffer if he doesn't come through. In this example, it might be that your computer is necessary to get a report in and maybe you'll get in hot water if it's not in on time—or something to that effect.

5. Seeing is believing: Real estate agents know the power of this tactic. When showing a home they want the people to *envision* it as theirs. Taking it from someone else's house to *their home* is a powerful visual technique. So when showing the customer around they'll ask questions such as, "Where do you think you might put the TV?" and "Where will the sofa go"? In this example you might ask your friend, "What will you do first? Hook up the monitor or go through the booklet?" You want him to "see" himself doing what he says he will.

Power Point

Master magician Harry Houdini offered a simple explanation when asked how he was able to so easily escape from a closed and locked safe. He said, "Safes are built to keep people from getting in, not to keep people from getting out." If you want to double-check to make sure that someone's truly committed then use this quick technique.

There is a psychological door that we keep guarded and tightly closed, but there's always a back door that we can walk right through. This *Back Door* tactic is a simple and highly effective questioning technique. It works because no matter how well practiced someone is at convincing you of his sincerity, he isn't prepared to respond to this tactic.

The key phrase is: "What would have to happen for this *not* to work out?" This is so effective because his entire line of thought is not on why he *wouldn't do something* but on why *he would*. He's used to answering questions as to why he is doing or will do what he says he will. But answering clearly what would *prevent* him from accomplishing his objective requires that he would first have to have *true intentions* of doing it. Put simply, it's asking him to think like a person who holds a different belief. Under normal circumstances—if he was honest in his intentions—this wouldn't be a problem, but it becomes one when an individual is not sincere.

After you ask this question the only answer you should expect is a fast "nothing" or a reasonable obstacle—something specific that is beyond his control. We all have reservations, and acknowledging them doesn't hamper our commitment. It just makes us honest. But if you ask Jake what would *prevent* him from marrying his girlfriend next year and he smiles and says, "I don't know . . . if things change . . . or something," Jake is not committed. If you merely ask, "You will marry Jane, right?" then he'll respond with a convincing yes, and give you all the reasons why he loves her. Because this is the question that he's been getting consistently and he can answer it easily and believably. The reverse, however, is not what he's expecting or is prepared for.

Strategy Review

✎ When you initially ask for the favor, hit as many of these five points as you can: (a) Get him to say it; (b) get a specific time frame; (c) develop a sense of obligation; (d) engage his conscience; and (e) have him tell you how things will unfold.

✎ Then end the conversation with a firm verbal confirmation and a simple phrase such as, "So I'll see you next Saturday, right?"

✎ Finally, as the day approaches let him know that you appreciate that he's someone who really follows through and/or that you are glad that he knows the true value of friendship/responsibility/loyalty—whichever best applies.

16

How to Get a Stubborn Person to Change His Mind About Anything

Fewer things can be more frustrating than trying to pry open the mind of a closed-minded person. But by following a precise set of psychological tactics you can get anyone to listen to what you have to say *objectively* and *fairly*. More than this, this strategy paves the way for getting someone to change his mind without a wall of resistance.

When you're dealing with a closed-minded person there are four possible factors for this attitude:

1. This person usually says no to everything, no matter what the idea is. If it's new, it's frightening and he doesn't like that. His motto is "change is bad."

2. This person has a problem with some people—in this case you. You find that no matter how persuasive, no matter how much your idea makes sense, if he hears it from you, he wants no part of it.

3. This person just came off another, though unrelated, situation, where he felt taken advantage of and manipulated, and the wounds are still fresh. Anything that further deviates from his usual thinking is not well received. He's not feeling good about his ability to make decisions and will retreat to safe ground to avoid being swayed.

4. This person has a *situational aversion*. This means that it's got nothing to do with you but "the whole idea" of whatever it is just doesn't sit well with him—meaning that "it's just not him." Your idea is inconsistent with his self-concept—how he sees himself.

If you've ever faced any people like this, you know that arguing with them will get you absolutely nowhere. The stronger your argument becomes, the greater their rejection of it. Logic goes out the window and nothing you say or do will make a difference. Unless, of course, you say or do the *right* thing.

If you believe that someone's resistance is due to either *A, B,* or *C*, then you'll simply use a two-phase process to get him to reevaluate his thinking about any belief, value idea, person, place, or thing.

Phase I: Various studies show that if prior to asking a favor, you can get a person to make a statement that is *consistent* with granting your request, you're likely to get a change of attitude and then her compliance. What you want to do is *have her agree to an idea or a way of thinking that will later neutralize her own objection.*

No matter what this person's attitude, you can adjust her thinking radically and quickly with just this one tactic. For instance, let's say that you want your boss to hear you out on a new idea. Simply say, "Don't you think that closed-mindedness is such an undesirable trait?" Then after a short time when you bring up the subject, you'll find her unusually cooperative and open to your suggestions. Because once your boss readily agrees with this statement she's unconsciously driven to act in a consistent manner.

This tactic is so highly effective because human beings have a strong need to be *congruous* with their attitudes, beliefs, and actions. For if someone thinks one way and does something else he's thought of as confused and nutty. And we perceive ourselves in the same way. Once we commit publicly to a stance, our attitude will conform to it and then influence our subsequent actions. As we'll see below, depending upon the situation, you can ask more *specific questions* to create greater internal consistency in a person.

Phase II: Restrict, in some way, or some part, his ability to do what he doesn't want to do. That's right. When someone is stubborn it's because he knows that he *can* do something but *chooses* not to. By thwarting his *ability* to do it the equation is now thrown off because he no longer sees the decision as his. *And if you can't do something, then you have no reason to be stubborn about it.* As a matter of fact, it *increases* the desire to do it! This instantly melts the wall of obstinacy. It's like telling someone who doesn't like to travel that she can never leave her town. Suddenly, with her freedom restricted, the ego goes into overdrive and creates an unconscious desire to *be able* to leave. Then once the desire to *be able* to leave kicks in, it's followed with the *desire* to leave because of cognitive dissonance. The thinking is, "I want to *be able* to leave because I must *want* to leave." The mind then begins to race for ways to do what it feels it must want to do.

This restriction can take any form. Why do you think coupons have expiration dates and sales are for a "limited time" only? If the option is always open to us, our impetus to act is not so strong. But once something becomes restricted—whether or not we really wanted it in the first place—we become more interested in it. Does prohibition ring any bells?

But here's the key: The restriction must be something that is overcome when *the person* comes up with the solution.

Now let's follow through with the previous example from Phase I. Let's say that the idea you want to put forth to your boss is that the office should have a company-sponsored picnic at the park next Friday. You think that your boss may be against that idea so you begin by laying the groundwork in Phase I with a general question, such as "Don't you think that closed-mindedness is an undesirable trait?" or "Don't you just hate it when someone won't hear you out on something?" Then follow up with a more *specific* statement such as, "How important do you think company morale is to an office environment?" These are obviously two loaded questions that once agreed with and expanded upon will produce an internal need for congruence.

Then you simply complete the tactic with Phase II, where you might say something like, "I'm sure that most people would love to go on a picnic, but I don't think that we could (a) get a park permit in time, or (b) decide on what sports to play so everybody's happy, or (c) get anyone to cover the phones." And that's all you have to do.

Now look what you've managed to accomplish. You had a closed-minded person who heard you out on your idea, agreed that it makes sense, and then proceeded to figure out how the suggestion could best be implemented.

This, done in conjunction with the following six power tips, will give you the opportunity to create a change of heart in even the most closed-minded person. These tips can be used as part of your two-phase strategy, though it's not necessary to employ them all.

Six Power Tips

1. When a person becomes adamant about his position, change the one thing that you can—his physiology. A person's emotional state is directly related to his physical state. If he gets locked into a position of denial or refusal, get him to move his body. This prevents what is called *mind-lock* and makes it easier for him to change his psychological position. If he's sitting down, have him get up and walk around the room. If he's standing, try to get him to sit down. When our *body* is in a fixed position, our *mind* can become similarly frozen. Numerous studies overwhelmingly concur that there is no easier way to snap anyone out of a mode of thinking than to *get him to move his body.*

 Power Point

The power of physiology on our emotions is startling. You can try this on yourself. Sit hunched over, legs drawn in; frown and put your head down. Stay that way for a few minutes. Now how do you feel? Chances are you feel pretty lousy. But now move around and wave your arms and shake and move your body. Notice how your entire emotional state changes. By bending and moving our bodies, our minds too become more flexible toward other ideas and ways of thinking. Have you ever given any thought to the belief that older people seem more set in their ways than do younger folks? Could it have something to do with the fact that as we age our bodies become less agile and flexible?

---

2. Give additional information before you ask someone to again reconsider. Nobody wants to be thought of as "wishy-washy," meaning that if he changes his mind without any new informa-

tion he may be perceived, and think of himself, as inconsistent. Rather, before asking him to agree, each time offer some other bit of relevant data or remind him of something he may have forgotten about. In this way he can make a *new* decision based upon *additional* information instead of simply *changing his mind.*

3. Studies show us that when our self-awareness is heightened we are more easily influenced. This suggests that when we can see ourselves—*literally*—in a reflection, we are more persuadable. Having a conversation by a mirrored wall or reflective panel will increase the chance for compliance.

4. Reciprocal persuasion: Cialdini, Green, and Rusch (1992) found that if someone had previously perusaded you to change your mind, he would be more inclined to *reciprocate* by changing *his* attitudes about something when you ask. Similarly, if you had resisted his appeal and not changed your mind, he would often "reciprocate" by refusing to change *his* own mind. You can use this very easily to your advantage by saying, "I thought about what you said regarding [any previous conversation where he was explaining his point of view] and I've come to agree with your thinking. You're right."

5. Studies conclude that when a person holds an opposing view, you should adopt a *two-sided argument.* When you're dealing with a stubborn person, we can likely assume that he's based his opinion, at least in part, on fact. Therefore, a one-sided argument will appear to him as if you are not taking his thinking into consideration. Consequently, in this instance, present both sides (following the rule of *primacy,* be sure to present your side first) and you will find him more malleable in his thinking.

6. Let him think that he is, in some way, *responsible for the idea.* This accomplishes several things; most important is that he will identify more strongly with the objective. In this way, his actions are deemed to be consistent with some aspect of his belief system. Once you've eliminated his resistance, you want to follow it up with psychological motivators to take action. To round out your strategy use the techniques in Chapter 13, Get Anyone to Take Immediate Action in Any Situation.

Now, that was the easy part. But remember that a few pages ago we said that there are *four* motivations behind stubborn thinking. The previous tactics covered reasons A, B, and C. But what if his stubbornness is due to D? (Remember that D is a situation aversion—meaning that this new idea is inconsistent with someone's self-concept—how he sees himself).

Getting someone who is closed-minded due to D to change his mind is going to take a different strategy. The reason is that when we are entrenched in a belief, it usually involves our identity. And that means changing our mind forces us to reevaluate how we see ourselves and how we look at the world.

This closed-minded person has *identified* himself with his belief and this is how he sees himself. By questioning his beliefs he is forced to bring his identity into question. For instance, let's say that you want your boss to move up your name on a list of executives in line for a bonus. He adamantly refuses because he considers himself to be a fair and honest person who would not corrupt the system. To do this for you would mean bringing his entire self-concept—how he sees himself—into question. No matter how strongly you argue your case, he's not budging because *it's not about you, it's about* him *and how* he *sees himself.*

No techniques of influence or persuasion will work unless you first address this issue. The key lies *not* in separating who he is from what he does. This is what we often try to do, but this person's anxiety will just increase the farther his actions move from his self-concept. Instead, this psychological methodology employs a technique to *merge* his self-concept and his behavior.

Let's continue with the above example where you want your boss to do you a favor that he sees as "nothing that he would do." Most of us consider ourselves to be good people. And it's safe to say, included in the definition, that we, of course, wouldn't kill another person. Yet, under what circumstance might you consider it permissible? If your own life or a family member's life was being threatened by a crazed gunman, perhaps? Now you *can* kill and still maintain a consistent self-image. *By changing the parameters you include the behavior to make it acceptable and even necessary.*

This tactic is made infinitely easier by using generic ideals in human behavior—which is the ideal way in which we all like to think of ourselves. To do this you just *align yourself with a greater and more important value* to which this person holds.

Under what circumstances might it become okay to move one executive's name ahead of another's on the list? It might be acceptable if this executive would suffer some sort of grave consequence if he didn't get the bonus. Now, so we're clear, you shouldn't fabricate the reason, nor do you have to. If you really need someone to do something then your real reason should prove to be all you need. And remember, it's not so much what the reason is, as long as you *present* it in the right way. And that is to incorporate your desire into his idea of morality and how he sees himself. You see, instead of trying to overcome his sense of decency, you simply *appeal* to it. Now we picked one of the toughest examples possible. It would be rare that you will have to contend with such an obstinate position. But when you do you'll be ready for it.

But wait, is there a way to tell just *how stubborn* a person is about something? Surely you can't change everybody's mind about anything? Well, there will be times when a person absolutely won't budge, so to save yourself some time and energy use the technique below to not only *determine* if he's movable but also to help you budge his thinking if he is at all flexible.

THE CROWBAR

Aren't there times when you would like to be able to tell if someone is willing to do something? How open-minded is she to trying something new? Have you ever wanted to know if someone was just putting up a strong front but could easily give in to your request? Try this *psychological crowbar* to open a closed mind and see what she's really thinking. This is the perfect test to tell how open-minded someone is. Furthermore, it helps to pave the way to getting her to embrace the idea in its entirety.

Sometimes people put up a strong front because they know that they will crumble if they ever have to defend their position. It has been said that the easiest people to sell are those who have a sign saying NO SALESMEN OR SOLICITORS. The reasoning is that these people know deep down that if a salesman did get to them they would buy whatever he had to sell.

With this technique you tell her that you want her to agree to doing what you ask, but *only if you can achieve some highly difficult and amazing task.* For instance, you tell someone to write down on a piece of paper a number from one to one hundred and if you can guess what it is then she will agree to what you want. She will likely agree because she believes that there is little chance that you can guess right. If she *does not* agree to these terms then it is likely that she is adamant about her stance.

The psychological strategy here is not in being right (if you are that's great) but in her agreeing to take the chance. Again, if at this point she absolutely refuses, then you know that there is no way that she is likely to comply. However, if she does agree then you've managed to adjust slightly her belief system—and this is all that you need. You take her from a no to a maybe. Now she will have to alter her belief system to allow the possibility—though remote—for this to happen. In order to reduce dissonance she unconsciously adjusts her thinking and will *now become more open.*

She also now believes herself to be the kind of person who takes risks—which is precisely the image you want her to hold of herself since your request falls outside of her usual comfort zone.

Only someone who would, in the back of her mind, be willing to do what you ask for will take part in this test. So some part of her, to some degree, is willing. Now you know that you're not dealing with an impossible task.

Strategy Review

- Begin with the Crowbar Test to determine just how closed-minded she really is.
- Because human beings have a strong need for consistency have her agree to a similar idea or a way of thinking that will negate her own objections later.
- Restrict in some way her ability to do what you want her to and give her the opportunity to provide the solution.
- A person's emotional state is directly related to her physical state. Change easily the one thing that you can—her physiology.
- She will be reluctant to change her mind without any new information because she will think of herself as inconsistent.

Give additional information before you ask her to again reconsider.

- Let her know that you've been recently influenced by her ideas. If someone is successful in persuading another person she usually reciprocates by changing *her* attitudes about something else in response to a persuasive appeal from that person.

- Adopt a two-sided argument to increase your credibility, being sure to present the evidence to support your position *first*.

- If possible show her how she is in some way responsible for the idea in the first place.

- Employ the tactics in Chapter 13, Get Anyone to Take Immediate Action in Any Situation.

- If the idea goes against her value system, change the parameters of the request, making the behavior acceptable.

17

Get Anyone to Do a Favor for You

How would you like to get complete cooperation from anyone in any situation? Well, now you can if you follow these sure-fire tactics for cooperation anytime, anyplace, for just about anything. These are the ten factors that influence whether somebody helps you out or politely (or not so politely) refuses your request. (If you're worried that once he agrees to help, he might not follow through, simply use the techniques in Chapter 15, Get Anyone to Follow Through on a Commitment to You.)

1. TIME COMPONENT

When is the best time to ask for a favor? Should you ask close to the time you want someone to take action or as far in advance as possible? The answer is *when the event is farther in the future.* As the event approaches the greater the anxiety and the "realness" of what he has to do sets in, and the less likely it will be for you to gain cooperation. If you need help with something right away though, studies suggest that you should find someone who is not rushed or preoccupied with something else. The ability to gain cooperation from someone who is not under a time constraint goes up dramatically, compared with someone who is preoccupied or rushed.

2. RECIPROCITY

Have you ever wondered why religious groups offer passersby a flower or some other gift in the airport? They know that most people who accept the gift will then feel compelled to give a small donation. We know we don't have to, but we can become uncomfortable, even though we didn't ask for the gift in the first place. When someone gives us something, we often feel indebted to that person. If you offer something, *anything,* to your target person you will significantly increase compliance. Your "gift" can take the form of your time, your attention, or even a small gesture or compliment.

3. BYSTANDER APATHY

Numerous studies in helping show that as the number of bystanders *increased* the percentage of individuals who helped those in need *decreased.* This is called the bystander effect whereby behavior is influenced by the *diffusion of responsibility.* This is true of almost all situations. When you want someone to do something for you let him know that you have no one else to turn to. If he thinks that you can go to anyone and that it's not up to him to be the good guy then his sense of responsibility is lessened and he doesn't feel any moral obligation to help out.

4. MOOD

Is it best to wait for him to be in a good mood before you ask? Not necessarily. There are actually slightly different dynamics at work, and hence strategies depending on his mood. Research shows that if he's in a good mood, you want to let him know *clearly* what you need for him to do and that *he will feel good about it in some way.* This is because positive emotions can result in *less helpfulness if the need is ambiguous or the consequences of helping are unpleasant.* When we're feeling good we don't want to lose our mood.

Studies also show that negative emotions can increase a person's willingness to help because helping makes people feel good and those in a bad mood are motivated to take action to make themselves feel better.

There are some exceptions here, but for the most part the required behavior has to be perceived as *relatively easy* and *effective* and it has to *seem clear that the helpful act will lead to more positive feelings.* So when he's not in a great mood, be sure to emphasize that what you want him to do will not take a lot of effort and that he will indeed feel good after he's done what you've asked of him.

5. Apathy or Empathy

If the person thinks that your situation is due to incompetence or ignorance, you will generate *apathy*, not sympathy. And if you don't have a person's *empathy* or *sympathy* it is much more difficult to get his help.

Studies show that you will increase your chances of being helped if your problem is not perceived as your own doing. This, by the way, is why so many of us are eager to provide help to a sick or injured animal—a dog for instance. We feel so bad because we know that *this was done to the dog* and that he didn't inflict it on himself. Contrast this with the oblivious attitude many big-city people have as they step over a homeless human being in the street. *He's probably on drugs, or a drunk, they may think to themselves. How did "they get themselves" into this mess?* When the individual is not responsible, we feel empathy, which motivates within us a strong desire to try to be helpful. You do this by making the person you want to help aware—if this is the case—that the situation you find yourself in was caused by *external events* and that you are in a sense *a victim* of the situation.

6. Similarity

Put simply, we tend to help more those whom we like and we like those who are *like us*. (For a more detailed explanation see Chapter 1, Get Anyone to Like You . . . Every Time.) The fact is that we are always more inclined to help those whom we like and we often like someone because he is "just like us" or is similar in some respects.

7. Internal Consistency

Fascinating studies regarding memory and behavior conclude that people often base their self-concept on *availability,* or how *easily* they can bring information to mind. For instance if you were asked to think of several times where you acted impulsively and were able to recall these events with relative ease, then you would see yourself— at least temporarily—as someone who was *impulsive*. However, if you had difficulty recalling times when you were impulsive your self-concept would conform around your inability to quickly access the memories and you would conclude—at both the conscious and unconscious levels—that you are someone who considers carefully before taking action.

And this rule of human behavior is pertinent because it coincides with the law of expectation: *We* act *in accordance with how we see ourselves.* You've seen by now, through the other chapters, the power of ego and our need for internal consistency with how we see ourselves and how we behave. So follow the logic through: If you change someone's self-concept then you change his behavior. And now we know how a person's self-concept is altered: *by the ease or difficulty of recall.*

Since we base our judgments on the ease of recall, you have the technique to change how somebody sees himself. Then his actions automatically align themselves with this revised self-concept. This is so powerful because it also engages a third law of *consistency.* Put simply, consistency is the unconscious desire of human beings to act in a manner consistent with their self-concept. For example, if you see yourself as a loving, caring person, it is almost impossible for you to act in a manner that is rude and obnoxious for any length of time.

Now if you want a high-strung person to be calm and relaxed, but you don't think that he will be able to recall too many times when he was calm, that's not a problem. Research shows that you can achieve the desired outcome—having him temporarily think of himself as a calm person—by having him elaborate on a specific time that he was calm. This is because he will paint for himself a mental picture of his state. And as the saying goes, "a picture is worth a thousand words." The *time* he spends remembering the event is a fair substitute for the *number* of times he experienced it.

Power Point

It's for this reason that some people have such a warped perspective of themselves. They have a computer-like memory when it comes to remembering their failures and mistakes in life: *so this is how they see themselves*—as failures. Even if our accomplishments far outweigh our mistakes, it's what we *remember*, the failures, that dictates how we feel about ourselves.

Getting someone to do you a favor is infinitely easier with this tactic because we act in accordance with how we see ourselves. And if you change how a person sees himself, then you can instantly change his behavior.

8. LEADING BY EXAMPLE

Knowing others "did the right thing" invokes an unconscious desire to do the same. It can actually lead to an increase in blood donations, as Irwin Sarason and his colleagues (1991) found after soliciting nearly 10,000 students at high schools. Students who viewed a slide show that mixed in thirty-eight photos of high school blood drive scenes were *17 percent* more likely to donate than those who did not see those pictures. Simply, viewing photos of people donating blood prompted more students to do the same than among those who did not see those pictures. Countless studies ranging from donating money to one's desire to help someone change a flat tire show this very same thing. The evidence is clear that prosocial models do promote altruism.

There will be many times when you simply aren't able to have someone witness others doing what you want him to do. And that's fine. Because you can enact this law *without* having this person actually witness another individual helping. And in reality, it can be more effective because as you read above in law number three, you want to avoid diffusing the social responsibility to act. Therefore, if someone learns of all those others who are helping, it may produce the opposite effect. Instead, use *metaphors* and *stories,* which are powerful tools of persuasion. Tell him of those who have helped in similar situations (it doesn't necessarily have to be this one) to produce the desired psychological effect.

9. THE EGO

Studies conclude that people are more inclined to be helpful to a friend if the friend's success *does not pose a threat to their own self-esteem.* This is why we might be more likely to help a stranger than someone we know. Make sure that the person doesn't feel threatened by you or that you are in some way in competition with her. Also, envy or jealousy at any level can inhibit an atmosphere of cooperation. Try to remove any element of competition between you. You want to promote a *you and me against something else,* rather than *you helping me to get what I want.*

10. THE POWER OF PERSISTENCE

Most people say no because they are resistant to change. *Instead of asking just one or two times, don't give up until you ask six times.* According to research, that's the magic number. Across the board most people will tend to agree to something *after being asked up to six times.* Of course some say yes right away or after just a few times but *keep asking.*

Power Point

Clearly he should care about you and the situation. And if you've done a good job with your tactics then he will. If, however, he still doesn't seem overly enthused about helping, research indicates that *when empathy is low we are more concerned with rewards and costs.* Therefore, if in the end he simply doesn't care, then you need to explain clearly what he will get in *exchange* for helping you. Now it's a simple matter of illustrating how the benefits of helping exceed the trouble involved.

Strategy Review

- If you need something done in the near future, ask when he is not preoccupied with something else. If it is for something that does not need to be done right away, ask for the favor as soon as possible, farthest from the time that he will have to do it.
- Engage the law of reciprocity by doing something for him. Your "gift" can take the form of your time, your attention, or even a small gesture or compliment.
- Avoid apathy by increasing personal responsibility. This is done by letting him know that you have no one else to turn to.
- Your request should contain three components: (a) specifically what you want, (b) how he will in some way feel good about doing you the favor, and (c) the relative ease with which he can accomplish the task.
- If your situation is due to your incompetence, you will generate apathy, not sympathy. Focus on any elements of your predicament that were *not* your own doing.
- Reshape his self-concept to include the idea that helping you is something that is consistent with who he is.
- Knowing others "did the right thing" invokes an unconscious desire to do the same. Have him witness or simply tell him about those who have helped in similar situations.
- Studies conclude that if she feels threatened by your success you will not get her cooperation. Explain the situation as the

two of you working toward a common objective where you both win.

- Most important is to *keep asking*. Many times people just say no because it's easy and they're used to it. Persistence in asking—in accordance with these laws—will give you every opportunity to gain cooperation.

- Finally, once he agrees to help, it's important that he follow through. Therefore use the techniques in Chapter 15, Get Anyone to Follow Through on a Commitment to You, to make sure that you get the help that is promised to you.

18

The Greatest Psychological Secrets of Leadership

Get Anyone to Follow You

You've got great ideas, a clear vision, and you're ready to change the world. One problem . . . you're leading but nobody's following. Leadership seems so easy to those who have mastered it, and so elusive to those who desire it. Effective leadership though is not so much an art as it is a science. In this chapter we explore the key essentials to turn anyone into a charismatic, passionate, and idealized leader.

Several factors make up the dynamics of effective leadership and they are divided into two main categories: The Personality of Leadership and The Mechanics of Leadership.

A: The Personality of Leadership

IDENTIFICATION

Effective leadership means thinking in terms of the *other person*. You can motivate any action in anyone if you appeal to her desires, her needs, and her wants. But before you do, bear in mind that *people do not care what you know until they know that you care*. People can sense whether or not you're walking your talk, and you cannot lead unless you truly believe. From the ancient classic *Tao-te Ching* by Lao-tzu comes this enlightening passage about leadership: "Evolved leaders win the trust and support of the people through their complete identification with them. The interests of the people are naturally promoted because they become the interests of the leader as well" (Wing, 1986). To accomplish *identification* you must not set yourself apart from the crowd, but remain one of the people *in the crowd.*

HUMILITY

It is not enough to be for the people; you must be of the people. An ego, contrary to what is often thought, is not what makes a leader great. We need look no farther than Mahatma Gandhi or Martin Luther King, Jr., to know that humility breeds followers. Again from the ancient classic *Tao-te Ching*: "When it is clear in their words and actions that leaders do not feel superior to those whom they lead, the people see themselves in their leaders and never tire of them" (Wing, 1986).

Those who rule with an ego rule with anger and fear and when those things are gone so too is their influence. History is full of these ego-oriented tyrants, dictators, and warriors. It has been said that the best person to lead is the one who has the role of leader thrust upon him, rather than one who seeks to rule because he desires power. Do not set yourself up as better than the rest, only as more *willing* than others to lead and as someone who is prepared to do what is necessary.

STYLE

Still, the most effective tool for influencing and leading can be summed up in one word: *simplicity.* Nobody likes or is overly inclined to follow complex and disorganized strategies. More wisdom from *Tao-te Ching*: "Leaders who impose elaborate strategies on people cause social reactions that undermine the structure of the organization because clever strategies strike a resonant chord in people and trigger their own cunning responses. If leaders, instead, guide the organization with simplicity and directness, the inherent cleverness of the people will be disarmed" (Wing, 1986).

Be clear and organized with your plan when you seek to inspire people to align themselves with your way of thinking. If your ideas are muddled with countless exceptions and are multifocused you will undoubtedly lose a person's interest and then his support. Be *clear*, be *simple*, and be *direct*. Please note that nowhere in here do I say to be rigid. If you are seen as unyielding you will be perceived as unreasonable and irrational. Maintain a degree of flexibility, but only when it makes sense, not when it's just easy.

PERSONAL POWER

So now you know the effective strategy for leadership, but as every good leader knows sometimes you need to be able to influence individual members to gain cooperation. So let's go a step farther and talk about how to present yourself as a *person* and as a leader.

Here are some crucial personal do's and don'ts to act the part of a responsible and authoritative leader. First, *never confuse passion with authority.* Don't be overly emotional. Emotion conveys passion, which is fine, but that doesn't give you an air of confidence or of authority. *Overly passionate leaders are believable but no one wants to follow them.* Second, never yell or raise your voice to anybody. This will cause you to lose respect. And if you cannot lead yourself then you cannot lead others. And if you cannot control others, then they have no reason to listen to you. Third, be respectful of *everyone.* By ignoring a person you do not show how big and important you are, but how small you are. By giving everyone respect and attention you gain the one incredible ingredient that is essential to every great leader: *charisma!* This elusive trait is gained by showing people how great *they* are, not by showing them how wonderful you are. People will follow someone who makes them feel good and valuable, not someone who makes them feel unimportant. Great leaders do not try to get the people to believe in them; rather they show the people how to believe in themselves.

Finally, numerous studies point out that when two people or teams work together toward a common goal the tension lessens. If there is infighting or lack of cohesion, they turn their attention to a common outside force. For further elaboration of this idea see Chapter 21, How to Get *Any* Group of People to Get Along.

B. The Mechanics of Leadership

Once you have the passion and the support of the people, you still need to gain unwavering commitment by applying psychological techniques. The most crucial ingredient in the leadership mix is knowing how and when to ask for input. Leaders are often made and broken depending on how they handle this issue.

The question is, *What level of participation is ideal for leadership?* Should you be running things like a democracy or a monarchy? The following study illustrates how a leader should conduct himself regarding participation of the group. Leaders who permit a fair amount of participation by followers will generally be more effective than leaders who permit either too much or too little participation (Vroom and Yetton, 1973). Other research shows that if the leader doesn't need his followers' support and can make decisions with his own expertise, he *should not* ask for help. If, however, he does need the people's support, then he should ask for it. A person's leadership style needs to be flexible so as to allow for the differences in these situations.

Strategy Review

- Leaders win the trust and support of the people through their *identification* with them. Do not set yourself apart from the crowd, but remain one of the people in the crowd.
- Humility is one of the most powerful character traits for effective leadership. A strong ego creates a barrier between the leader and the people.
- Your vision must be clear, simple, and organized. Nobody likes or is overly inclined to follow complex and disorganized strategies.
- Don't confuse passion with authority. Overly passionate leaders are believable but few people want to follow them.
- Never yell or publicly chastise anybody. This will cause you to lose respect.
- Instantly generate the often-elusive and ever-important quality of charisma by making *others feel important and special.*

People follow those who make them feel good about themselves.

✎ Understand the mechanics of leadership and when it is best to ask for input and when it is best to dictate.

19

Get Anyone to Understand Anything

The Two Greatest Secrets to Explaining Anything Complex

If you want someone to agree to something or to take action, the first rule is that he should understand exactly what it is that you're talking about, and precisely what you are asking of him. It can be quite frustrating explaining something over and over again. But by incorporating these two tactics you can pretty much explain anything to anyone.

First, the person should know the *context* of the information. To explain easily a hard-to-understand point, you need to offer perspective by first explaining the entire picture.

Give him an overview so that he understands the context of the situation. For instance, you can listen to and memorize a sentence because you know and understand what the words mean. But ten random words such as *bat, go, fly, how, to, starter, never, hot, tremendous,* and *hen* are difficult to keep in your head. A cogent sentence, however, with ten words in it is infinitely easier. *The four boys were reading Shakespeare in the corner room.* You can repeat this back and memorize it with great ease. But how long might it take you to memorize those ten random words above? The sentence is easier because you understand the order and context of the words and how they relate to one another.

Explaining details and specifics without first making sure that someone understands the concept, the larger picture, is like putting a puzzle together without knowing what the picture is. Those who don't have a strong understanding of something usually don't have a concept of the larger picture.

The second factor in making sure that you are understood has to do with *expectation*. Numerous studies show the powerful role that expectation plays in understanding and include such findings as (a) girls who were told that they would perform poorly on a math test did so; (b) assembly line workers who were told that the job was complex and difficult performed less efficiently *at the same task* than those who were told that it was easy and simple; and (c) adults who were given fairly complex mazes solved them faster when told that they were based on a grade-school level.

Our own expectations and the expectations of others play a powerful role in how we digest information and consequently on our performance. If you want someone to understand something, explain the context in which the information fits in and communicate the fact that you expect him to understand it, and that it is simple to learn. Additionally, offering positive encouragement along the way will help to maintain his enthusiasm for learning and understanding. If you follow this approach you will greatly increase anyone's ability to understand, use, and retain any information.

Strategy Review

- Give an overview before going into the details. This puts the new information into an understandable context.
- Use the law of expectation. Simply stating that you expect this information will be understood quickly and easily greatly increases comprehension and retention.

20

Minority Rule

How to Get Your Way
When Everyone's Going the Other Way

History is full of examples of those whose thinking shaped the future. Unyielding as they were unconventional, these visionaries helped shape a world not yet born. And these free thinkers were not part of the collective thought of mediocrity but were men and women who flew in the face of tradition and in doing so paved the way for change, for progress, and for liberty. Men and women who fervently believed in a good and righteous cause, never yielding to fold into the middle, rose against insurmountable odds to speak their passion and stir a society of conscience.

But what if you just want sushi and everyone else wants Italian food? No problem, you can get your way. When you're outnumbered and outvoted, this tactic will sway the majority to your way of thinking. Whether you want your ideas implemented at the office or you want to see the movie no one else wants to, you'll find this method very useful. And whether you've got one ally, ten, or none, these rules of human nature are strategized to help you influence forces greater than your own. (Techniques in Chapters 14 and 16 to get anyone to take your advice and changing a person's mind certainly can be used to round out your overall strategy.)

There are *six main elements* that determine how effective you will be in swaying the majority to your way of thinking. They are outlined and explained below.

1. CONSISTENCY

First, you and/or members of your group must be *consistent* in the opposition to majority opinions. Studies show that if you waffle or show signs of giving in to the majority view your impact is reduced. In other words, a statement such as, "Based upon all of the information, we stand one hundred percent behind our position," is in accordance with this law. The statement, "Hmmm, I don't know . . . no, it's just better this way . . . yeah," is not suggested.

2. FLEXIBILITY

Studies show that the members must avoid appearing rigid and dogmatic. A minority that holds to the same position regardless of new information and a changed situation is not as effective as one that demonstrates some flexibility. This does not contradict the previous law. Within a single position you should remain unified and unyielding, but when presented with new evidence or a unique situation, you should take the time (or at least appear to do so) to consider this and weigh it, without casual disregard. A statement consistent with this rule would be, "That's an interesting thought that has not yet been considered. Why don't we take a short time to determine its merit?" An ineffective statement would be something such as, "No, no, no . . . I don't care! That's where we stand and that's that."

3. DIVIDE AND CONQUER

Many studies conclusively prove that when we have an ally we are much more likely to stick to our guns. That means that if Jim knows that Bob is against your idea too, he'll be much harder to sway. Yet, if Jim thinks he's alone in his thinking, then not only is he more likely to change his view but he will agree to things more easily if he thinks that the whole group is for that way too. Don't let them gain confidence in their numbers. Speak and sway individually whenever possible.

4. LIKABILITY

As a function of discord, when you disagree with the majority you are often perceived as less friendly and may be disliked. Being liked is more times than not an essential component of influencing people. So the secret is to point out how your view is in the best interests of others, not just yourself. Applying the tactics in Chapter 1, Get Anyone to Like You . . . Every Time, will also stem the tide of losing popularity.

5. NEW ANGLES

Whenever you want someone to reevaluate his thinking, remember to *introduce new information* into the equation. In this way he's making a *new decision* based on *additional information*. This is easier for him to do than for him to "change his mind." A good way to use this phrase is, "I understand why you thought this way, but we just found out that [new information]. In light of this new information, maybe we could approach this in another way."

6. OUTSIDE SUPPORT

Now, what do you do if nobody's budging? When you've got nothing, enact the law of *social proof* by finding other people, outside your group, who share your view. This will make your group more inclined to reevaluate their thinking. You're having trouble finding *anyone* to support you? No problem, just find an expert or others to agree with you that *don't* have a personal stake in the situation.

When college students received a compelling message supporting a departmental exam *before* graduation they found strong arguments more convincing than weak arguments. No surprise here. But when the same message would have no effect on the students—advocating that the exam policy begin in ten years—the *quality of the argument made little difference.* The *expertise and credibility of the source,* however, did matter (Petty, Cacioppo, and Goldman, 1981).

So when you don't have a winning argument, try to get support from those who are not directly affected, as these people are prone to pay less attention to the quality of your points.

Strategy Review

🖊 You and/or members of your group must be *consistent* in the opposition to majority opinions. Do not show signs of waffling.

🖊 Avoid appearing rigid and dogmatic. In light of new information, a minority that holds to the same position regardless of the situation is not as effective as one that demonstrates a degree of flexibility.

⚓ Divide and conquer. Many studies conclusively prove that when we have an ally we are much more likely to stick to our guns.

⚓ When you disagree with the majority you are disliked, hence making it difficult to sway them. Applying the tactics in Chapter 1, Get Anyone to Like You . . . Every Time, will give you the edge.

⚓ Don't ask someone to change his mind without introducing additional information.

⚓ When you've got nothing, enact the law of *social proof* by finding other people, outside your group, who share your view.

⚓ Read Chapter 18, The Greatest Psychological Secrets of Leadership, to make your argument as powerful and persuasive as possible.

21

How to Get *Any* Group of People to Get Along

Whether it's bickering friends or a feuding family, these techniques will quickly melt away disagreement and provide a core of unity among all members.

Numerous studies conclude that division among people dissolves when there is an opposing outside threat. External events arouse our need for affiliation and we will seek out support, creating a heightened sense of unity. Civil warring, intersocietal conflicts, and internal unrest often cease when a common outside enemy comes on to the scene. Conversely, individuals will turn their attention and hostility on one another when no outside forces are present. The fastest way to instill cooperation within a group is to (a) create an external threat or (b) simply set your group against another group in some form of competition. A common enemy brings opposing sides together faster than any other type of group cohesion technique.

This phenomenon is also characteristic of how people respond within their own lives and minds. When your mind has nothing to focus on it divides against itself and creates a breeding ground for worries and anxieties. Yet, once you get a clearly defined outside goal that you are passionate about these divisions cease. Have you ever noticed this to be true in your own life? When you have a clear-cut objective, you're in a better mood and your attention is clear and focused. Suddenly the "little things" don't seem as important to you anymore. You have perspective on what really matters.

A mind, like a group, with nothing to occupy it, will turn against itself. When we have nothing to focus our attention on our mind creates its own unrest and fears begin to take root. But as soon as there is something of interest that absorbs our attention, our mind quiets.

This is why many people find hobbies so relaxing. Our focus is external and our mind becomes absorbed completely in something and we lose ourselves, as it were. It's for this reason that those who have nothing going on their lives are often the most neurotic. Without an external focus to occupy their attention their mind begins to turn in on itself. But once an objective is created our attention is turned outward. So too do groups who are confronted with a serious issue find that infighting quickly gives way to this new objective.

Also interesting is a study done by Ross and Samuels (1993) who found that the *name* given to a game has *greater influence* on the level of competitiveness than the individuals' personalities. They found that when participants played a game they believed to be called Wall Street they were much more competitive than their counterparts playing the same game, believing it was called Community Game. This is so fascinating because something as seemingly minor as the name of the game can override the members' personalities. Therefore, we can reasonably conclude that *within your group* careful consideration should be given to the name of subsets as well as the overall group name. For instance, if you have two sections of your group with names such as The Righteous and The Victors, chances are you won't be inspiring as much cooperation as with names such as Common Ground and The Flexible Thinkers.

Power Point

The strategies outlined above will help you to keep the peace and maintain unity and cooperation. But while doing so, you may find a person or two whose personalities just seem to clash with others. With them, it's important to observe three other rules for cohesive cooperation to ensure the peace.

✔ Arrange opposing parties so that they are next to each other, not across from one another. When we are opposite one another physically, our position becomes more entrenched as we begin to develop an "us against them" mentality. Side-by-side sitting promotes the optimum atmosphere for unification and cooperation.

✔ Contact and proximity: Keep the parties close and in constant contact with one another. As we've seen through numerous studies in this book *proximity increases liking*. You want to be mindful not to keep everyone on top of each other, but a degree of closeness is essential for maximum cooperation.

✔ Touch. Never underestimate the power of the human touch. If possible, try to create a situation where members can shake hands or come into contact with one another. Touch increases greatly our feelings of intimacy. We feel more connected psychologically to those whom we touch physically.

Strategy Review

🖉 Numerous studies conclude that division among people dissolves when there is an opposing outside threat.

🖉 Make sure that your group identifies itself with an image that is consistent with a spirit of *cooperation*, not *competition*. The *name* given to your group or clique greatly influences levels of cooperation.

HOW TO WIN AT ANY COMPETITION: BEAT OUT ANYONE FOR THE JOB, THE DATE, OR THE GAME

There's an amusing story about two men who are out camping in the jungle when one of them spots a ferocious lion. One man kneels down and takes his running shoes out of his knapsack and begins taking off his hiking boots. "What are you doing?" exclaims his friend. "You'll never be able to outrun the lion." To which the man calmly responds, "I don't have to outrun the lion, I just have to outrun you."

Even when you're dealing with good, honest, and decent people, there are times when it's going to come down to you against him. These psychological tactics will show you how to make sure that you come out the victor in any battle, be it a physical competition or a battle of wits.

22

Secrets to Winning in Any Competition
Strategies for Beating Anyone at Anything

Whether it's a battle of the mind or of the flesh, the strategies are almost identical. This is because all battles are first waged within the mind; it is there where you win or lose and then the outcome is manifested into the material world. Whether it's a tennis match, a spelling bee, or two men vying for the attention of a woman, *competition is competition. Attack the mind of your opponent* and you will divide him against himself and then he will fall before you, without a single touch.

You don't have to be the best or brightest in order to win, *you just have to do the right things.* Whether it's a physical battle or a contest of minds, it is the one who is *mentally prepared* and who psychologically strategizes that will win time and again. While the situation will dictate how many of these tactics are appropriate, any combination will prove to give you an overwhelming advantage.

There are two different areas of strategy to successful warfare:

1. You: SECRETS FOR BEING THE PERFECT PSYCHOLOGICAL WARRIOR

◆ *Anchor in success.* As we talked about before, anchors are often used in hypnosis to link unrelated events or sensations. To review, an anchor is an association between a specific set of feelings or an emotional state and some unique stimulus—an image, sound, name, taste, etc. We see examples of conditioned reflexes in our own lives. Perhaps the smell of vodka makes you sick because you had a bad experience with it several years ago. Or a certain song comes on the radio and you recall a friend you haven't thought about in years. These are all anchors. In much the same way that a stage hypnotist is able to snap his fingers and have a person fall asleep, you can "lock in" a certain behavior.

You can use the power of anchoring to *enhance* your *performance.* Let's say you're playing tennis. Anytime you make an exceptionally good shot, repeat a short phrase to yourself, or make a quick gesture with your hand. This is the anchor to your action. Then, when you want to perform in that optimum state, simply repeat the phrase to yourself or make that gesture and it will throw your brain right back into the same frame of mind you were in when you were at your best. This is a highly powerful tool that when used correctly will allow you to, at any time, enter your peak state of mental and/or physical performance. You can *condition yourself* to perform in an optimal state at will. Whenever you're performing in the zone and at peak performance, anchor your state and then fire it off whenever you want to perform at maximum efficiency.

◆ *Focus.* Here's an undeniable fact about human nature: What you focus on is what you will move toward and for. Never, *ever* act out of fear. Remember that all significant battles are first waged within the mind. If you don't feel that you're mentally ready and at your best, and if you can delay, then *don't* take action.

◆ *The ideal state.* Your ideal state of mind is to have *no ego* and this is achieved by *focusing solely on your objective.* This will allow you to be unconcerned with how you are coming across and help you to avoid second-guessing yourself. If you are absorbed with your objective the "I" or the ego disappears and you can pursue your goal relentlessly. Focus only on the outcome, not on yourself.

◆ *Mentally rehearse.* See and feel what you will look like and act like in your ideal state. When it comes to performance, studies suggest that mental rehearsing can be *just as effective as actual practice*. Use your mind to get the perfect image of how you would like to perform. What do you sound like and look like? What is the reaction from others? How do they see you? Have a complete picture of exactly how you want your reality to unfold. You have to see yourself succeeding in your *mind* before you can see it with your *eyes*.

◆ *Always have a plan B.* Not only will your perspective be healthier, but you will also increase your chances of success. The challenge in doing this though is that you don't want to set yourself up for failure by abandoning your original plan too quickly. So go to plan B *only* if your original plan is impossible to execute. In the armed forces, during an attack, if something goes wrong, they *always* have a contingency plan to move forward. Remember, no matter what happens if you are prepared you can always move forward.

2. THE BATTLE: USING PSYCHOLOGY TO GAIN THE WINNING EDGE

◆ If a shark and a lion are in a fight which would win? It depends of course on where they're fighting. Whenever possible, get the home field advantage. You will be more comfortable, and your opponent less, in surroundings familiar to you. Whenever possible, spend some time in advance at the location where the "event" will take place so you can become more comfortable with your arena.

◆ Social facilitation is the *arousal* that results when other people are present and our performance can be evaluated; *studies show this arousal enhances our performance on simple tasks but impairs our performance on complex tasks.* These studies further illustrate that when you are skilled at something, complex or not, having people around helps your performance. When you lack confidence and are not skilled, then you will perform worse with others watching. When you are competing against someone who is more adept than yourself do it without others around. However, if you are more competent then have people around to watch because it will help you to perform better, and your opponent will do worse.

◆ To summarize one of history's greatest warriors and strategic leaders, Sun Tzu, whenever possible *do the unexpected and give no warning*. Deception and surprise are key principles to confuse your opponent. By acting without a pattern you throw him off balance and *this is when you want to attack the hardest*. When attention is scattered your opponent's focus is not clear. And by attacking first you have more options. Offense is dynamic, defense is passive. When you do attack, do not let up. Wear down your enemy mentally. A constant sustained barrage will tire him out by draining him mentally and physically.

Strategy Review

   ✐ Get the home field advantage whenever possible.

   ✐ Have others watch when you feel that you are more competent than your opponent. When you are less confident, try to compete without an audience.

   ✐ To enhance your performance, anchor your successes so you will be able to go into your ideal state at will.

   ✐ Never act out of fear, focus on the objective, not on yourself.

   ✐ Mentally rehearse your performance and desired outcome.

   ✐ Always have a backup plan. If your tactics are not working, make sure that you can easily switch to a new game plan.

   ✐ Do the unexpected and give no warning. By acting without a pattern you throw your opponent off balance.

23

The #1 Mistake Most People Make in Life

It's the Biggest Mistake Gamblers Make Too!

The way people gamble and how they live their lives often parallel one another. Because, really, life is a series of decisions and gambles, and what we decide to risk, and the outcome that follows, often determines the kind of life that we have. Many people systematically make the same mistake in life and we can look at it clearly by taking the example of gambling.

Casinos work on a percentage of as little as 2 percent for games like blackjack and baccarat. Some of the games—depending on the gambler's skill, or lack thereof—can give the casino a margin as high as 20 percent or more. So why is it that on a typical day *80 percent of the people will lose money?*

The stock market has two directions it can move in: up and down. Conventional wisdom suggests that you have a fifty-fifty chance of winning or of losing. Yet, *90 percent* of the people who play the market daily—by themselves, without outside input—will, over time, lose. Why? It's not because of the odds; *it's because of their strategy.*

GAMBLER A: THE CHASER

Here is a typical scenario of Gambler A. He bets $10 and loses; he bets $10 again and loses; now he bets $20 and loses; $30 and loses. He *increases* his bets as he does worse. The gambler tries to chase his money—trying to win it all back in one hand by betting more to make up for the times he's lost.

Gambler B: A Man Divided Against Himself Will Fall

Here is a typical scenario of Gambler B. He bets $10 and loses; bets $10 and loses; after some time his bet goes down to $5.00 Good plan? No, because he never feels successful. If he wins the $5.00 bet then he feels he should have bet more and if he loses then he still lost. And he's partly pleased he's lost because it is through losing that he can now justify to himself lowering his bet!

And what about when we're winning? Another reason why casinos have million-dollar marble chandeliers in the lobby is not because of government subsidy programs; it's because *gamblers don't know when to stop.* The longer you play the better it is for the house. When you run out of money you'll stop. But when you're winning when do you stop? Often you don't, since there's no reason to, so you keep going until the tide turns against you, you lose, and then you are *forced* to stop.

So if increasing your bet when you're losing isn't the answer and decreasing it when you're losing isn't the answer, what is? Research suggests that when you are losing you should do what gamblers hate to do—*stop.* However, when you are winning or on a "streak," then it is a fair strategy to increase slightly your amount of play.

One other interesting fact to note is that all unsuccessful gambling strategies are predicated out of fear. When you act out of fear your decisions are not logical, but *emotional.* And this will ensure that you will end up on the losing side of the game. *Never do anything out of fear.* If you *need* to win then you will lose. You must only focus on the game, not the outcome. If you are praying to win then you are fearful of losing. The best mentality is that of pure detachment—where you're completely objective and unemotional. If you're gambling with money that you cannot afford to lose it is impossible to remove the emotional element from your decision-making process.

Can you recall those times when you were completely in the zone? You may remember that fear was absent. It was just pure action, where you weren't even aware of yourself, just what you were doing. That is how you win in gambling and in life. As the saying goes, he who cares less wins! If you are fearful, wait until you are more confident before proceeding. If you don't feel like it, don't do it—or you will lose. As we've seen, our strategy when we gamble is almost identical to how we handle situations in the real world. So by changing your tactics you can go with the *odds* instead of your *emotions,* and come out a winner just about every time.

Strategy Review

✐ When things are going your way—when you're in the pattern of success—it makes sense to put more on the line and slightly increase your risk. And when you're going strong, *you* decide when to stop; don't be forced into early retirement. But when things are going against you, stop and regroup.

✐ Never do anything out of fear, if you can avoid it. Fear clouds your thinking and places your focus on the negative outcome. If you need to win then you will lose because you will be focused on what is at stake and not on the objective. Detach yourself from the objective and get in the zone before you take action.

Section V

MAKE LIFE EASY: LEARN HOW TO INSTANTLY TAKE LIFE'S MOST ANNOYING, FRUSTRATING, AND DIFFICULT SITUATIONS AND GET THE UPPER HAND EVERY TIME!

This section contains the greatest psychological strategies for handling life's most trying times and circumstances. If you want to simplify your life or just plain make things easier then these tactics will be invaluable for you. For life's little tribulations and uncertainties, you'll learn *exactly* how to make sure that things go *your* way . . . every time.

24

Get Anyone to Return Your Phone Call Immediately

There are several different strategies that people use to get their messages returned. The least successful but most often used ploy is the "this is really important" message. It sounds something like this: "You'd better call me back . . ." or "This is an emergency . . ." These messages only manage to annoy and needlessly worry the person being called. Of course the situation will dictate the type of message that is most appropriate, but the following phrases are the very best psychological tactics to get anyone to return your call. They appeal to a basic aspect of our primal nature: curiosity.

1. I found out and it's not too late! When you call, I'll fill you in.
2. I'm so excited for you. Give me a call, we'll talk about it.
3. I owe you this much. When you call me I'll fill you in.
4. You were right. When you call me, we'll go over it.
5. I know you're going to love it! When you call, I'll tell you how.

But what message will get your phone call returned faster than any other? Leave these sixteen words on any machine or with any secretary and wait for your phone to ring.

"I appreciate what you've done. . . . Please give me a call. I'd like to thank you personally."

This is the entire message. The person called knows that with a message like this, it's problem free—no headaches or explanations. It blends *curiosity* with *gratification*. It shows that you're a nice person for acknowledging what he's done (whatever it is), and that makes him feel good: to be appreciated. Most important, it's confusing. No matter how enticing a message is, if it's clear what you're talking about, the person will always make the decision as to whether or not it's *important enough* to return your call. If, however, he's not able to make the decision because he doesn't have enough information, as is the case here, then he can't conclude that he doesn't have to call you back. Have you ever gotten a confusing message on your machine mixed in with a bunch of regular messages? If you have, you might recall that the one that makes no sense is the one that makes you want to call back first to find out what is going on—because it *may be important.* If a person understands the message, then he can conclude on his own whether or not it's important. And you don't want him to do this.

The unknown is what needs to be clarified. It's for this reason that many people will disrupt an enjoyable telephone conversation with a good friend to answer an anonymous call-waiting beep. Why? Because they don't know who it is, and it may be important! The unknown beckons us. Since you want your message returned, you have to say who you are, of course, but as for the rest of the message, leave them wondering. Combining all of these factors into one message is the sure-fire way to get anyone to respond.

 Power Point

If you're calling a company, ask the person who answers the phone whether the company uses pink or white message pads. (Almost every company uses one of these colors.) When she responds, say "Okay, can you do me a big favor? Can you draw a smiley face next to the message for me?" You will be absolutely amazed at how many people comply. Then when the person you left the message for is sifting through his messages, it's the one with the smiley face that's going to get his attention—especially coupled with the message that you left for him.

Strategy Review

➤ Leave a message that in some way shows your appreciation, but isn't clear as to what it's about. Human beings have an inherent curiosity, and by not making your message clear, it forces the person you're trying to reach to clarify what it's about.

25

Get Anyone to Forgive You for Anything

Okay. You've screwed up, you feel guilty, and you've promised never to do it again. If that's enough to set things straight, terrific. However, we both know that sometimes it takes a lot more than "I'm sorry" to make things right. Let's see how we can use psychology to help you get forgiveness, *fast*.

The psychological strategy in seeking forgiveness for cheating on your spouse is of course going to be different than if you were late for a meeting with your boss due to a traffic accident. (Also, the tactics vary depending upon whether it's your *behavior* or your *words* that got you in trouble. First, we'll look at correcting *misdeeds*; then you'll see how to gain forgiveness when you *misspeak*.) In instances where your intentions were good but outside influences interfered use the following.

Research suggests that if your excuse is due to *circumstances beyond your control* it is received much more favorably than an excuse that mentions only *reasons* that you had control over (Weiner et al., 1987). For instance, simply saying that "you didn't feel up to it," or that "you completely forgot," will likely generate unnecessary hostility and anger toward you. However, if a six-car pileup on the freeway or a flat tire is the culprit, you will be more readily forgiven. The reason for this is that nobody wants to feel as if she is being taken advantage of, or think that you didn't "care enough." Therefore, by placing the blame on an outside source you remove the attitude that leaves her feeling angry and unimportant.

So if your mistake was beyond your control, let the person know this. One caveat is that you also need to let her know that you *planned* for this possibility, but were unsuccessful. For instance, if traffic caused the delay, you want to cut her off at the pass because she may be thinking, *You knew this was important to me, so why didn't you leave more time?* When explaining the circumstances also include the fact that you *anticipated* the possibility of this problem—in this case heavy traffic—but it was *much greater* than you could have reasonably prepared for.

One other thing to keep in mind is that your apology should be *sincere* and *specific.* It's been shown that giving a specific accounting of the circumstances involved, as opposed to vague generalities, is highly effective in reducing a person's anger (Shapiro, Buttner, and Barry, 1992). *It's all in the details!*

This should suffice, but if it doesn't you can proceed to the tactics below, which are designed for more severe breaches of trust and consideration and when the circumstances were *not* beyond your control.

When you've done something wrong, this person feels violated in some way. There is a sense of betrayal. She feels you don't respect her enough, you don't care, you're not interested in caring, etc. Therefore simply saying, "I'm sorry," doesn't correct the situation because you haven't *restored her sense of dignity.* Your actions took away some of her power. To make her feel better you need to return her psychological state to the way it was.

Below is the framework for a four-phase process that will ensure your success in achieving swift and complete forgiveness.

PHASE I: RESPONSIBILITY, APOLOGY, AND SINCERITY

Unlike the previous situation, here it is important for you to take full and complete responsibility for your actions. Do not shift blame or assign excuses; this will only exacerbate the situation. The person is expecting you, to some degree, to lay the blame onto others. This doesn't help because if the blame is placed somewhere else *then only that other thing or person can restore that person's sense of importance.* If *you* take responsibility then you have the power to set things right. Again, balance must be restored to the person's ego. She needs to know that she was not taken advantage of and that her feelings were considered.

Next, apologize for your behavior. Occasionally we forget to actually say the words, "I'm sorry." While just these words often aren't enough, they are essential to your overall strategy for gaining forgiveness. Sometimes it's very hard to say this, but as hard as it is, it is that much more important to gaining forgiveness.

Finally, make sure that your sincerity comes across. Any apology that is not sincere will not be believed. And if you are not believed then you will not be forgiven. If you're not truly sorry, then you will likely do what you've done again and put this person through more pain and sadness. So if you don't mean it, don't say it. If you're not truly sorry and remorseful it might be time to reevaluate the relationship or situation.

PHASE II: REMORSE AND PUNISHMENT

A very important phase in this process is to let her know that you are *willing to face and accept any and all consequences for your actions.* An apology without remorse is like a sports car without fuel: It looks great but doesn't *do* anything. Showing remorse gives her back the one thing that she lost: *power.*

She will likely do nothing or much less than if you never put your fate in her hands. But remember your fate (at least with her) rests in her hands at this point anyway. But freely giving her the power—and acknowledging it as hers—to determine your fate is extremely important. She wants justice for what you've done. She wants to be able to exercise her rights as a human being and be given the respect she deserves. Give her back what you took and you will be forgiven. You can start by saying something such as "I know what I did was wrong; you have every right to be angry with me. I'm willing to accept the consequences for my actions."

 Power Point

Even in court cases, studies show that if you don't show remorse then you are likely to receive a higher sentence. You need to restore the balance with your words or you will be *punished* as a way of setting things straight. It is in balance that we find justice. And in justice that we find forgiveness.

In extreme instances it may be necessary to employ the following technique, which will allow you to rapidly diffuse her anger. Here, you go a step further and actually *suggest a punishment*— the harshest one you can think of. She will then be forced to talk you out of it, because she will likely feel that even *you don't deserve such a harsh penalty.* And in doing so she inadvertently creates an effect in psychology called cognitive dissonance. (This is characterized by an anxious state, which arises when an individual holds two conflicting attitudes or ideas. To reduce the anxiety, this person has to justify the inconsistency.) Once she talks you out of your actions she has to reconcile that what you did was not "as bad as she thought" as a way of unconsciously making sense of her mixed feelings. In other words, she unconsciously rationalizes to herself, "If what he did was so bad, why would I talk him out of that punishment?"

PHASE III: DUPLICATION AND EXPLANATION

So far the previous tactics have you above water, but if you want to reach dry land, you'll need to go farther and implement the following.

Explain to her how the set of circumstances that created this event *can never happen again.* Part of her disturbance over your behavior is the unpredictability of your actions. That is, it's something that has happened and can happen again without notice or warning. If you can assure her that the combination of events can never repeat itself, then this will go a long way toward alleviating much of her anxiety. By isolating the event you minimize its impact on her life as an anomaly and not something that she will ever have to deal with again.

Now is the time that you have to answer "why?" Her entire world has been upset, nothing makes sense, and you have to give her a *plausible explanation* as to why you did what you did. She will not be satisfied and is unlikely to be able to let it go unless she understands *what* led to your behavior. A simple "I don't know" or "I wasn't thinking" will do nothing to allay her fears of a repeat performance.

But here you run into a challenge—one that usually sinks most people who have gotten this far. How do you explain your actions without sounding like you're defending them? This is the last thing you want to do.

The very best way to explain your actions is to *root them in fear.* Whether it's personal or a business situation, you're still dealing with human beings. And all people understand fear. It is primal and pure (e.g., "I was *scared* because things were going so well"; "I *feared* that you would fire me if I didn't lie about the warranty"; "I lied because I *feared* you would hate me if you found out the truth").

Now your actions are seen less as a betrayal that violated trust, and more as an irrational act of fear by a confused person. It *furthers your vulnerability,* and helps to restore her feeling of power and dignity. *By assuaging your fears she takes an important and active role in restoring her own sense of control.*

Remember that the objective is to restore the sense of balance and this, in conjunction with the other tactics, does just this, because rooting your motivations in fear diminishes the perception of your ego. Simply, fear is a response to feelings of your inadequacy to deal with the situation. This is in stark contrast to a braggadocio, self-centered mind-set—one that you do not want to present.

 Power Point

Have you ever wondered why after someone cuts us off on the road we often do two things? One, *become angry,* and two, *try to see what this person looks like.* First, we're angry because we weren't "respected" by this person and second we want to see what he or she looks like to determine if the individual looks like the kind of person who would do this to us on "purpose." A little old lady doesn't enrage us as much as a young male might. This is because we assume that she cut us off by accident and that it's not personal. The totality of your responses is ego-based. Someone did something to you and you're angry.

PHASE IV: NOTHING TO SHOW FOR IT

Finally, it's important to let her know that your actions produced no enjoyment, financial gain, or any type of benefit whatsoever. Since no one can go back in time, you need to relay that not only was it a *mistake* but that it didn't *produce the anticipated benefits.* Remember, the key to forgiveness lies in restoring balance to the relationship—be it personal or professional. If you gained in some way, then you will have to "give back" more in order to set things right. Never acknowledge any benefits (external rewards) or satisfaction (internal rewards) from your behavior. For example, you want to say things such as "The sex was lousy"; "I never spent any of the stolen money"; "I was more miserable and so filled with guilt afterward"; etc.

This strategy will set into motion her forgiveness. Now you have to wait for the only thing you can't manipulate: *time.* Once sufficient time passes, all of the elements will fall into place and your life as you knew it will once again be restored.

Power Point

The above are behavioral misdeeds, but sometimes it is our words that wound. These are simple enough to deal with using a technique called *globalizing*. For all those who have put their foot in their mouth one time too many and who speak without thinking, this technique will save you a lot of energy and heartache.

IN PERSON

If you offend her directly, oftentimes a quick "just kidding" doesn't do much to assuage her hurt feelings. Therefore you should do what's called *globalizing* the comment *as soon as you say it*. For instance, you're arguing with a coworker and you tell her that she's completely incompetent (oops!). Right after you say that you need to employ damage control: ". . . along with everyone else in the damn company." We are offended by something in great part due to our taking it personally. This add-on diminishes the impact. This way it's taken as one complete belief and it dissipates the personal impact. Instead of feeling hurt or that there's something wrong with her, she will probably think that you need a vacation.

THIRD PERSON

If your words get twisted or you unintentionally offend someone, globalize your words and put your statement within the context of a larger point. For example, "No, I didn't say you were driving *me* crazy, I said *everyone* was driving me crazy." Since she's hearing it third person, there's usually enough doubt to throw you into the clear.

Strategy Review

- ✐ If your explanation is due to *circumstances beyond your control* it is received much more favorably than an excuse that mentions only *reasons* that you had control over.
- ✐ If the situation was not beyond your control—meaning that it was completely your own doing—then make sure that you take *full* and *complete* responsibility for your actions.

✐ Your apology should be *sincere* and *specific*.

✐ Let the person know that you are prepared to face and accept any *consequences* for your actions, and that your fate is in her hands. You must restore her sense of power.

✐ Demonstrate how the set of circumstances that led to your behavior can never occur again in the future.

✐ If fear was part of your motivation, be sure to explain exactly how your actions were rooted in this fear.

✐ Show that your actions did not produce any of the anticipated gain or benefits.

26

The Best Way to Break Bad News

How to Get Anyone to Take Bad News as Well as Possible

Life can sometimes deliver to us the unkindest of blows. When you are in a situation where you are to be the bearer of bad news, this strategy will benefit you greatly. You are about to see that you can dramatically alter how a person responds to *any* situation by *changing the way you deliver the information.*

Language has a powerful impact on how we perceive and consequently *feel* about what we hear. This is often why good salespeople know they shouldn't say, "*Sign* the *contract.*" Instead they suggest that you, "Okay the paperwork." Even though you're doing the same thing, you don't feel as comfortable *signing the contract* because it's been imbedded into us ever since we were little not to sign anything and to have a lawyer look at any contracts. But *okaying the paperwork,* that's something you can do without worrying.

Cult leaders know the powerful impact of language. In 1997, thirty-nine members of the Heaven's Gate cult took their own lives in a mass suicide. In reviewing videotapes the members made before their deaths, we repeatedly heard the cultists refer to their bodies as a *container.* It is much easier to destroy a "container" than it is your body. Over time they gradually began to accept the idea that their bodies were merely a container, and therefore of little importance or value. This is why it became so easy for them to "dispose" of the container and kill themselves.

Power Point

Politicians understand well the power of words to influence attitude and behavior. People are more comfortable hearing about a *military action* than a *war* even though they mean the same thing. We would rather hear of *collateral damage* than be told that *civilian property was accidentally destroyed;* and we are not as disturbed hearing of *friendly fire* as we would be to hear what it really means—*our soldiers shot at our own forces.* And, of course, watching the morning news we are less moved being told of *casualties,* than we would be if the reporter said what that meant: *deaths.* Most of know what these words "really mean" but, again, that doesn't matter. It's how we *digest the information,* and language is essential to that process.

Language alters our perception of reality because *we see the world through words.* Language is the basis of thought and thought is the extension of emotion. Therefore, you can substantially decrease a person's reaction to a situation by choosing the right words. So what are the "right" words?

You want to avoid harsh language. *Don't use words that have a strong negative connotation.* Doing so avoids an automatic reaction—like we often have to signing contracts—and helps the information to be processed and internalized more slowly. In much the same way that a body goes into shock if there is an overload of pain, the mind is similarly shocked. However, if we receive the information in smaller intervals (using softer language) the "shock" is diluted and that helps to severely lessen the impact of the news. We say "time is the great healer" because it is the *suddenness* of negative information that amplifies the pain. The passage of time allows us to put things into proper perspective. When something first happens we have no perspective because it is in the present. It is all-consuming.

Let's say that you just found out that your nine-year-old son took the family car for a joy ride and was brought back by the police. You might be understandably upset. However, instead, what if you just found out that your nineteen-year-old son took the car *ten years ago*? In both scenarios you *just found out the news* but your reaction is entirely different. Why? Because of a perceived passing of time. Time is a powerful psychological tool that can dramatically shift our perspective.

 Power Point

Language also alters our perception of how we *remember* things. Research by Loftus (1979) in eyewitness testimony shows us that how the question is *phrased* can substantially impact on how we *remember* the details. For instance, regarding a traffic accident, those who are asked how fast the car was going when it *smashed* into another car give higher "estimates" than those who are asked how fast the car was going when it *hit* the other car.

How we deal with information is also influenced by our belief system. Whatever beliefs we hold about a particular situation dictate how we will respond to it. For instance, some cultures believe that a birth is a joyous event, so they celebrate it. And they believe that death is not good and so at funerals they are sad. But some cultures believe that death is a glorious transformation, an event to be celebrated, and they are joyous at funerals. Notice it is not the event, but our *beliefs* regarding it, that determine how we feel. All information—specifically sad and bad news—is a function of a specific set of beliefs.

When a person becomes upset about an event in her life, it's because of one or more of three cognitive beliefs: (1) she feels that the situation is *permanent*; (2) she feels that it is *critical*, meaning that it's more significant than it really is; and (3) she feels that it is *all-consuming*, that it will invade and pervade other areas of her life.

When any or all of these beliefs are present it dramatically increases our anxiety and despondency. Conversely, when we think of a problem as *temporary, isolated,* and *insignificant,* it doesn't concern us at all. By artificially deflating these factors, you can *instantly* alter a person's attitude and make it more positive. Certainly the type of news will dictate how this can best be used, but if you can address at least *one* of these you will be effective in diminishing the unpleasant reaction.

It's also so important to keep in mind that when information is at all ambiguous or has vague implications we often don't know *how* to respond. We take our cue from others. For example, if you're in a crowded movie theater and somebody yells "fire," how might you respond? Research tells us that if the rest of the audience sat in their seats, you would likely remain seated as well. But if there were a mad rush for the exit, it's likely that you too would begin to leave.

When we are unsure of what something means, we look to our world to provide us with information on how "upset" we should be. The more relaxed and assured *you* are in relating the news, the calmer *she* will be.

Another psychological technique, which is part of your overall strategy, is based on the *law of contrast.* This law states that we don't think and see something as it is, by itself, but in relation to other things. In essence we *contrast* and *compare.* (This phenomenon is discussed in more depth in Section I.) By contrasting the situation with something worse it's perceived in a new light and in a better perspective. For example, if you bring your car to the mechanic and he tells you that you need new brakes, you might be appropriately displeased. However, if he were to first tell you that you might need a new engine, a new transmission, and a new exhaust system, only to inform you an hour later that you just need *front brakes,* your thinking may be, "Whew, I got away lucky this time." It's not the information itself that is so crucial, but rather the *context* of it and how it *relates* to everything else.

Let's take an example that incorporates some of the above tactics. Although it depends entirely on the situation, the following strategy will greatly reduce the psychological impact and pain. In this scenario a physician determines that his patient has diabetes. Look at the difference in the approach, and decide if you were the patient, which doctor would you rather hear the news from?

DR. A

Mr. Doe, *I'm sorry* to have to tell you this news, but *you have diabetes.* My laboratory tests *confirmed* this just *now.* And as you may or may not know it can be *life threatening* and you can face *severe complications* like *amputation* and *blindness. Everything* in your life has got to be *changed* from this second forward—what you eat, how you exercise, and so on. I'm truly *very sorry.*

DR. B

Okay, *you're in good health* except for a *variance* in your blood sugar levels. *I'm pleased* with these results and that *you came in when you did* because *it could have* turned into something much worse. You're in *good company,* too, there *are millions of other folks who have diabetes*; that's the technical name for it. And the best news is that it's *completely controllable* and when properly cared for *you won't even be aware of it.* As a matter of fact, *I think you've had this for quite some time* and you'll see with an improved diet and exercise program you'll have *a lot more energy and vitality.*

As you saw, both doctors delivered essentially the same information, but Doctor B gave the news in smaller increments which allows for the person to begin to accept the idea, mentally digesting the situation and hence, significantly *lessening the impact.* He used softer language and conveyed that there were positives to the situation such as improved overall health. His entire tone was positive and he said phrases such as "I'm pleased we caught this . . ." instead of "I'm sorry . . ." Of course the patient will need to be informed of other details, but in time. And once the newness is digested more information can be taken in without the usual shock and accompanying depression.

Strategy Review

✎ Avoid words that have a harsh, negative connotation or stigma. Language is the basis of thought and thought is the extension of emotion. Therefore, you can substantially decrease a person's reaction to a situation by choosing the *right words.*

✐ Present the situation when possible (or aspects of it) as *temporary, isolated,* and *insignificant.*

✐ Use the law of *contrast* and *comparison* by illustrating how it could have been worse than it actually turned out.

27

Get Back Anything You've Loaned Fast, and *Without* an Argument

Many of us have had the experience of loaning something out, whether it's money, a chain saw, or whatever, only to feel uncomfortable when asking for it back. Of course the obligation shouldn't fall on you to get it back; the person you've loaned it to should return it without your having to ask. But when he doesn't, here's how to get back anything quickly and easily. (By the way, if you have trouble saying no when asked for things, read the next chapter and *never feel guilty again!*)

The first stage of this technique is simply to ask for it. Sometimes the direct approach works best. And be sure to include a valid reason as to why you need it back *now.* For instance, "Sam, that two hundred fifty dollars I loaned you last week I need back because I have to pay off a bill that comes due tomorrow." Simple, direct, and to the point. And if we lived in a perfect world this would be enough, but we don't, so often it isn't.

If this doesn't work then you need to create more leverage. Since someone has what you want you need to up the ante and *appeal to his ego.* This can be done several ways. The following strategies can be used in order and until you meet with success. As you will see if you meet with resistance the tactics increase in severity.

1. Tell the individual that you know her to be the kind of person who does the right thing. In fact, that's something you admire most about her. This statement brings her self-worth and belief system into the equation (we've covered this in detail in previous chapters). Now by not giving you back what she borrowed she risks having to reevaluate her self-concept and how she

sees herself. You might say something such as, "You know, Samantha, what I've always liked about you is that you try to do what's right and fair." Then in a few hours simply ask for your money and she's going to be unconsciously motivated to do what is "right and fair."

2. With this technique you appeal to her sense of dignity. Tell her that a few people you both know (in shipping/on the block/at the salon—you need not mention names) told you that you would never get it back. You might say, "I don't want them to be right about this; it'll make us both look foolish." This makes her feel as if everybody is talking about her and she's going to want to institute damage control—and that means giving you what she owes you.

3. If this doesn't work then you need to use more severe measures. You do this by saying that you're going to have to tell others about this so they won't lose money to her as you did. Most people will do anything to protect their public image, especially something as simple and easy as giving back something that they've borrowed.

Strategy Review:

- Simply ask for it, being sure to include a *reason* as to why you need it back now.
- Tell her that you think of her as the kind of person who always tries to do the right thing.
- Appeal to her sense of dignity. Tell her that a few people you both know told you that you would never get it back.
- Tell her that you're going to have to tell others so they won't lose anything to her as you did.
- Remember too that people do favors for those they like. And yes, some consider giving you back what's owed to you as a favor. If the above don't get you anywhere see Chapter 1, Get Anyone to Like You . . . Every Time, to ensure your success.

28

Say No Without Hurt Feelings or Guilt

"No" is a complete sentence—so say it. But if you think that by saying no you're headed for an argument, use the following technique. It is one of the very best psychological tools and will save you much grief and aggravation.

There's a rule of persuasion called *reciprocity* that basically says, when someone does a favor for us we often feel the need to reciprocate. We've mentioned this before, but briefly; it's the same reason why religious groups offer a flower or some other gift in the airport. They know that most people will feel compelled to give them a small donation. We know we don't have to, but we can become uncomfortable, even though we didn't ask for the gift in the first place. When someone gives us something (i.e., time, information, a gift, etc.) we often feel indebted to him. This is also why so many of us have a hard time not buying something in a store after the salesperson *"spent all that time"* with you. It just makes us more comfortable to reciprocate in some way—in this case by buying something. Most salespeople are well aware that if they invest a lot of time with you, showing you a product, demonstrating how it works, you will feel somewhat obligated to buy it, even if you're not sure that you really want it.

Well, this law of reciprocity can be applied in the *reverse*. The technique works like this. When you turn down the favor (that's being asked of you) *ask for a favor* from that person right after you say no to his request. By asking a favor of him, which he most likely won't or doesn't oblige, you've in effect canceled your debt *as soon as he declines your request.* In much the same way that buying a shirt balances out the salesperson's investment of time with you, there is an unconscious feeling that balance is restored. You say no, he says no, and because of this, almost magically, he feels *okay* about it.

For example, a friend calls you and asks if he can borrow your car.

You respond with "Oh no, I can't because I've got to use it, but I'm glad you called. Is there any way you can walk my dog while I'm out of town next week?" Now he has to apologize to you and offer an excuse as to why he can't do this favor for you. This works great even on those people who try to "guilt" you into things. They will have a hard time arguing with you after just denying *you* a request. It will make him feel extremely awkward and usually too uncomfortable to press you on his favor. *Note:* Make sure that the favor you ask him for is something that he can't come through on. Although, you could ask for something really outrageous that you would like him to do for you, in which case if he does agree to it, then you might not mind doing the favor that he's asking of you.

Here's another fascinating and effective addition to this technique. Notice the use of the word "because" in the above example—it's there for a reason. A study done by Langer, Blank, and Chanowitz (1978) found that the word "because" holds an astonishing power.

Asking to cut in front of people using the copying machine, Langer's collaborator said, "Excuse me, may I use the Xerox machine?" to which a little over half of the people agreed. The fascinating thing is that Langer found she could get *almost everyone to comply* when they changed the phrasing of the request to: "Excuse me, may I use the Xerox machine *because* I have to make copies?" The reason was nonsensical. Of course you need a copying machine in order to make copies. So why does it work so effectively? Because the word *because* triggers an unconscious acceptance that a valid explanation will follow. We hear something and we have almost a Pavlovian response to accept it. Whether the sentence makes sense or not, we assume it does and, therefore, we don't bother to process the explanation.

So when you want to say no, simply say it, use the word *because*, and ask for a favor afterward. The conversation will end with no hard feelings and with you feeling great.

Power Point

If you're not sure if you can help out, don't say that you're not sure or that you'll think about it. The smartest thing to do when initially asked is to give a resounding, "Yes!" If you *can* follow through that's great, but if you can't, the other person at least knows that you tried because you initially agreed with such enthusiasm. Therefore, the reason you can't come through is not because you didn't *want to* but because you were just no longer *able to*. It starts at the beginning when you are first asked. If someone asks you for a favor say, "No problem," right away. That way if it turns out you can't oblige it won't seem as if you're looking for an excuse.

Strategy Review

- When you turn down the favor (that's being asked of you) *ask for a favor* from that person right after you say no to his request. By asking a favor of him that he can't come through on, you've in effect *canceled your debt* as soon as he declines your request.

- When you turn down his request, and before you ask him to do something for you, use the word *because* in your excuse. The word *because* triggers an unconscious acceptance that a valid explanation will follow.

29

How to Turn a Rude and Obnoxious Person into Your Best Friend

Win Over *Anyone* in No Time!

Whenever someone acts rudely or cruelly to you it's always because of one of four reasons. First, she thinks you dislike her; second, she feels threatened by you; third, she acts cruelly to everyone; and fourth, you've given her a reason to dislike you. If four is the case, then see Chapter 25 on getting someone to forgive and forget. If it's one, two, or three, read on for a terrific and highly effective psychological strategy to adjust anyone's attitude toward you.

First, make sure the problem isn't yours. By this I mean that research shows us that a person with a positive self-image tends to assume that others will respond kindly to them. And the reverse is also true. Those with a poor self-image tend to believe that other people simply don't like them. (Since they don't like themselves they feel that other people dislike them for the same reasons.) Therefore, if you have a negative self-image, this is what could be causing your belief that you are disliked. If this is the case there are several great books on developing positive self-esteem.

Moving beyond self-image, if you *expect* someone to dislike you—independent of how you feel about yourself—she usually will fulfill that prophecy. Even if you have a healthy self-image but *believe* that a certain person doesn't like you, you are likely to *perceive* this person as behaving in a way consistent with your beliefs. Additionally, your expectations may even *cause* her to behave in this way. Expectations play a powerful role in how our relationships unfold because as we've seen throughout this book people will treat you the way that you expect that they will. Make sure that it's not your attitude or false beliefs that are causing the rift.

Assuming your self-image, your beliefs, and your attitudes are not the problem, then consider the following research in this area for a rock-solid game plan for turning anyone into your best friend.

Many studies indicate that once we discover someone likes us, we tend to like him or her as well. This is what's known as *reciprocal affection.* We tend to *admire, respect,* and *like* someone once we are told that they have these same feelings for us.

Now what's the best way to communicate your affinity for this person? *Tell a third party,* maybe a mutual friend, that you honestly *like and respect* this person. Once this information makes its way to the other person, you will simply be amazed at how fast she comes around. Whether it's a coworker, boss, assistant, or neighbor, everyone needs to feel appreciated. Let this third party know how you genuinely feel about this person and watch the magic happen.

You may be thinking, "Why can't I just go and tell her myself? Why all this cloak-and-dagger stuff with a third party?" Well, there are actually two reasons you don't want to tell her yourself. One is that you run the risk of her thinking that you're insincere. When you hear something from a third party we rarely question that person's veracity. This is because the thinking is, "What's she got to gain by lying to me?"

Another reason why it works better via a third person is because of a quirk in human nature as illustrated by the following study. People with a positive or moderate self-concept respond to others' liking with reciprocal liking. But people with a negative self-concept respond quite differently (Curtis and Miller, 1986). Just as your self-image will distort how you believe others see you, her self-image will distort how she sees you. If she thinks of herself as not being worth very much or even unlikable, your kind words will seem unwarranted and she probably won't respond. While simple logic might conclude that a person who feels "low" would relish somebody liking her, you have to get past her mental barricades, which is, "Why is this person being so nice to me? What's wrong with her?" However, by not bringing up your fondness for her directly, you bypass this negative barrier.

If she sees you as a threat, then her dislike is rooted in jealousy and envy. You can dissolve her negative attitude in a similar way, with just a slight variation. Here, you want to focus on how you *admire* her for who she is and what she's done. It is very difficult for anyone to dislike you or to treat you poorly once she knows that you respect her. By letting her know (again via a third person) that she has your respect, you align yourself with her and she sees you as an ally and not as a threat.

Okay, you use the third party tactic to turn her around, but when you do run into her do you just make small talk? Talking about the weather isn't a bad choice, but if you really want to make an impact then use the oldest rule of getting anyone to like you. It comes courtesy of Dale Carnegie, who was one of the greats in understanding human nature. On the occasions where you do speak with this person keep this next sentence in the front of your mind! *Become interested in other people and you will get them to like you faster than if you spent all day trying to get them interested in you.* And it's dreadfully easy to get a person to go on endlessly about herself. Just ask questions about her and the floodgates of conversation will open.

But now a one-sided conversation is more of a monologue than it is a dialogue. So when you do offer up information about yourself remember this rule of human nature. We like people who not only *like us* but who *are like us*. If she discovers that you both share similar beliefs or ideas about something you will have created a psychological bridge that will make her feel closer to you and respond more favorably.

And above all, remember that someone likes you based not on how he feels about you but on *how you make him feel about himself.* You can spend all day trying to get him to like you and think well of you but it's how you make him feel when he is around you that makes the difference. Whatever the dynamics of the relationship, by making him feel comfortable, welcomed, and relaxed you will go a long way toward developing a good, true, and lasting friendship.

Strategy Review

✎ First make sure that *your* attitude is not the problem. If you expect someone to dislike you, you will likely interpret her actions through this warped perspective.

- ✎ Tell a *third party* that you genuinely like, admire, and/or respect this person. This will engage the law of reciprocal affection.
- ✎ By showing an interest in her you will get her to like you faster than if you spent all day trying to get her interested in you.
- ✎ Talk about those things that you *share* and have in *common*—ideas, values, thoughts, etc.
- ✎ She likes you based on *how you make her feel about herself.* You can be the greatest person in the world, but she will dislike you if you make her feel unimportant and insignificant.

How to Stop a Rumor Before Your Reputation Pays a Price

Would you like to defend yourself without getting defensive? Would you like to turn around false accusations and use them to your advantage? Now you'll be able to stop a rumor dead in its tracks, and gain leverage with this sure-fire psychological tactic.

Rumors thrive in *secrecy* and *anonymity*. This means that gossip survives because by its very nature it's told in "secrecy." If you expose the source then the well dries up. The gossiper, in most cases, is not likely to spread rumors once she is exposed.

This study illustrates the effectiveness of this tactic—how physical anonymity lessens inhibitions. Zimbardo (1970) dressed New York University women all in white coats and hoods. They were asked to give "electric shocks" to a woman. (Of course the shocks weren't real, but the participants believed that they were.) They pressed the shock button *twice as long* as did another group of women who were *not* masked and were wearing clearly visible name tags.

It's also easier to do harm to those *whom we do not see as real people,* and to those whom we *do not physically see* as well. In war, dropping a bomb on a city can carry less psychological trauma for a pilot than shooting a single man at point-blank range can carry for a soldier. Several parallel experiments show us just this: When we are removed from the person—when we do not see him *and* he is far away, *physically*—we are more willing to inflict physical pain. This also holds true for inflicting *psychological pain,* as in the case of making slanderous statements. Notice that there are two separate psychological criteria. One is that of *sight*—can we see this person—and second is that of *proximity*—how near is this person physically to us.

These studies, and many like it, depict three separate strategies for halting gossip. First, go to the source or to anyone responsible for the rumors and identify that person. Let her know you are aware of who she is and what she is doing. Second, you want to humanize yourself to this person as well. Let her know that there is a real person behind the rumors. Third, do this in person, when at all possible. The actual proximity—the closeness—makes a big difference.

Okay, so this works fine when you know the source, but what if you don't? What if there's just some rumor floating around and you don't know how it got started or by whom? Or for that matter, what if you *do* know the person and she just doesn't care about what she's doing to you and the damage done to your reputation by these rumors? For these instances, the following psychological strategy is an incredibly effective method of damage control.

There are essentially two characteristics of a rumor that dictate whether or not it spreads like wildfire or simply fizzles out. The reason rumors spread is that they are *interesting* and that they *sound believable.* It's been said that a partial truth is more dangerous than a total lie. That is because nobody gossips about what is obviously false and blatantly stupid, but with a grain of truth, it becomes plausible and that is what makes it interesting to talk about it.

But you can use this to your advantage. Instead of trying to deny, defend, or minimize the rumor, which can make people believe it more, simply spread a more outrageous rumor that *overshadows* that one, but *incorporates* it as well. For instance, let's say that a rumor going around is that you've been stealing from the company. Denying it can just make you "appear" guilty. Instead, you should spread the rumor that you used the "stolen money" to support your thirty-six adopted children or you used it to buy a seat on the space shuttle. Now this newer more salacious rumor is harder to believe and casts doubt about the accuracy of any of it. Most people will dismiss it as false if it doesn't *sound plausible.* They would have no reason to pick it apart to find the grains of truth if the whole thing just sounds made up. This is because rumors are seen in black and white as either true or false. Since there is rarely material evidence in a rumor, each person decides whether or not it makes sense. So the more outrageous it is the less sense it makes and the *less interesting* it actually becomes. The rumor gets diluted in a stream of obvious untruths, buried under an avalanche of nonsense. Nobody knows what to believe about whom.

So if going to the source doesn't work, simply extend the current rumor to include completely outrageous information and the whole thing will just be seen as silly.

Strategy Review

- ✎ If you know who is responsible for the rumors, go to her and let her know that you are aware of who she is and what she is doing.
- ✎ You want to humanize yourself. Let her know that there is a real person behind the rumors.
- ✎ Instead of trying to deny, defend, or minimize the rumor, which can make you appear more guilty, simply spread a *more outrageous* rumor that *overshadows* that one, but *incorporates* it as well.

31

Stop Verbal Abuse Instantly
Get Anyone to Sit Down and Shut Up!

When someone is rude to us our first reaction is to protect our ego. We respond with something such as, "How dare you talk to me like that"; "I don't like that and now I'm upset"; "Don't yell at me"; and so on. *We make this angry person our problem.* Why should you let someone else dictate how you feel? To get angry would be to give another person control over your emotional state. That's a lot of power for one person to possess, especially someone that is rude to you. This is more than just pie-in-the-sky self-help talk; there's actually a powerful psychological component to it.

If you resist your initial inclination to get defensive you may be surprised at what happens. Instead of, "Why are you treating me like this?" try saying instead, "*You* seem to be having a rough day." Rather than, "I didn't do anything, don't talk to me like that," say, "This seems to have upset *you*." *Don't take possession of his problem.* It's his problem, not yours. The psychological dynamics change dramatically as soon as you use the word "I" or "me." Then it becomes something between *you* and *him.* By using the word "you," you keep the ball in his court and the problem remains his sole property.

Aside from not upsetting yourself, you've now forced the person to think and respond defensively, in effect explaining *his actions to you.* You don't force him to find reasons to support his claim—that you've done something wrong. Instead you ask him *what's wrong with him, not you!* And let him spend all day on this.

You will find that by not responding defensively you won't become as upset by the exchange—because it has nothing to do with you *as long as you don't try to take part ownership of it!*

If this abusive behavior is a part of a larger pattern and you have an ongoing relationship with this person, take a look at the following. At the core of interpersonal relations is the truth that a person will treat you the way that you train him to. You need to let him know that his behavior is unacceptable and will not be tolerated. So the first thing you want to do is to call his attention to his behavior and let him know that it is not acceptable. In a perfect world this would be enough . . . but we don't live in a perfect world. So let's look at why he does this and what you can do about it.

He treats you this way because it makes him feel powerful. If you are worried about your physical safety then acknowledge his "authority and power" to diffuse his anger. To do this simply say, "You're right, I'm sorry." This magical phrase usually shuts down the verbal stream of venom. Then remove yourself from the situation and contact the appropriate authorities. If the above isn't working fast enough, you can use this tactic: *Become more upset at yourself than the person is.* He is yelling because he wants you to feel as he does: angry, hurt, frustrated, and *small.* So if you make him believe that you feel worse than he does, he accomplishes nothing more by yelling. When you beat yourself up he has no reason to continue kicking. When the tirade is over, leave and give serious thought to the relationship.

Strategy Review

- Resist your initial inclination to get defensive. *If it's his problem don't make it yours!* The psychological dynamics change dramatically as soon as you use the word "I" or "me." Then it becomes something between *you* and *him.*
- If you are worried for your physical safety then acknowledge his "authority and power" to diffuse his anger. Do this by becoming more upset at yourself than he is at you.

32

Get Anyone to Open Up to You
Get Specific Information from Anyone

Isn't it annoying to ask a question only to get a vague or apathetic response? I suppose. You get an answer, but it doesn't have any useful information in it. The following psychological tools allow you to easily narrow a vague response to give you a more direct, truthful answer. Here are some examples of how you can distill ambiguity into specific, detailed, and usable information. Notice how much more effective the "b" technique is than the traditional "a" response.

- I a
COMMENT: I don't think the meeting went very well.
RESPONSE: *How come?*
COMMENT: I just don't, all right!

- I b
COMMENT: I don't think the meeting went very well.
RESPONSE #1:   *How do you know when a prospect is interested?*
RESPONSE #2:   *Did someone say something or was that your impression?*
RESPONSE #3:   *Were you having an off day or were they just not qualified?*

If you ask for clarification, the person feels obligated to respond. Asking a broad question in response to a general statement just produces more of the same.

■ II a

COMMENT: I don't know if I could.

RESPONSE: *What do you mean, you don't know?* or *Why can't you?*

COMMENT: I just don't know, all right?

■ II b

COMMENT: I don't know if I could.

RESPONSE #1: *What, specifically, prevents you?*

RESPONSE #2: *What would have to happen for you to be able to?*

RESPONSE #3: *What would have to change if you did?*

You'll notice in the above that sometimes the person herself hasn't given it much thought. So by asking these questions you allow her to better understand her own thinking, which in turn, of course, gives you a clearer, more concise answer.

No one likes to be put in a situation where they feel they have to defend themselves. As a result, oftentimes when you ask someone what she is thinking or how she feels, she replies, "I don't know." This response can stall a conversation and leave you searching for answers. Sometimes it's just easier to say, "I don't know," which is often why we say it in the first place. If you answer her with "How come?" as is traditionally done, you'll often get an "I don't know" right back. Either way, when you hear, "I don't know," use these techniques to get the information that you want. (Pick the ones most appropriate to the situation.)

- "Okay, then why don't you tell me how you've come to think the way you do?"
- "I know you don't know, but if you were to guess, what do you think it might be?"
- "Can you tell me what part of this you are okay with?"
- "In what past situations have you felt similar to this one?"
- "What emotion best describes what you're thinking right now?"
- "Can you think of just one reason?"
- "What one word comes closest to describing what you're thinking?"

In all of these responses, you're taking the pressure off. You acknowledge the person's difficulty in answering. You then seem to be asking her to provide something else, when in reality your new question is aimed at getting your initial question answered and opening up the discussion toward a meaningful dialogue.

An "I don't know" could also mean that the person feels guilty or foolish about her actions. In this case you want to *relieve her of the responsibility*. This psychological technique is great because it allows her to answer truthfully without fear that you will judge her. *After all, she may believe that she didn't do it on purpose*. This works well because she doesn't have to feel responsible for her actions. It was not her "intention" to do what she did. Her behavior was not consciously motivated. Your phrasing might sound something like, "I know you're not sure about why you did that, so can you think of any *unconscious motivations* that may have been at work?"

Strategy Review

- When you get a vague answer, ask a more specific question that is related to his answer. If you ask a general follow-up question you will only get another general response.
- If the person is unsure of how to answer, ask her instead to tell you how she feels about an aspect of the situation, instead of the entire situation itself.
- Ask her if there might have been any *unconscious motivations* at work. This alleviates the element of guilt as it does not imply that there was intent.

33

Deal with Any Complaint Fast and Easy
Get Anyone to Stop Whining!

Whether it's personal or professional, follow this list of tactics and you can be sure to assuage anyone's complaints about anything.

First *listen*. Surprisingly most people don't know how to do this. To listen you simply say nothing and do nothing other than listen. That means you don't agree, disagree, or argue. In the next step you're going to agree, but if you do it right away, you risk his thinking you're just placating or patronizing him. *So let him say everything he wants to say without any interruption* and *then* agree.

Sometimes people just need to get something off their chest. So let them speak. Other times they're looking for a fight. If you don't interrupt, then they will eventually run out of things to say. If you interrupt you are going to give him more ammunition and risk a heated argument instead of a monologue.

Nobody wants to feel he's been manipulated or taken advantage of. And that is 99.9 percent of the reason why he is so angry. His ego has been damaged. Somebody or something didn't respect him enough and he is hurting. When he is done speaking do the following.

First paraphrase back to him what he's said, so he knows that you've been listening. Then build him up with phrases such as, "No one as important as you should have to go through this"; "I know you're not accustomed to being treated this way"; or "If I were you I would be just as upset." This completely takes the steam out of his tirade. The last thing you want is to be combative and with this first step you disarm him completely. You've made him feel important by listening, agreeing, and stroking his ego. Using this three-step process of listening, agreeing, and stroking will often diffuse the situation. But if it doesn't continue with the following.

Now, ask him what he would like you to do. What he offers as a resolution or solution is often much less than you would have given to compensate him for his troubles. In business situations we often make the mistake of wanting to give the world to avoid a bigger problem. But hold off on your initial temptation and ask him what he would like you to do.

In personal situations, complaints may come the way of vague statements, such as, "I'm not happy," or "You're driving me crazy." While there may be more serious relationship issues at hand, there is a specific way to help the situation. What you want to do is have him get as specific as possible about what is bothering him. (See Chapter 32, Get Anyone to Open Up to You, on how to turn a vague answer into a specific response.)

While you're doing the above, try to establish rapport to get him to like you and to calm him down. The way you present yourself can greatly influence the attitude of the other person. If, while he's venting, your arms are crossed and your posture says, "When are you gonna shut up?" you're heading for a confrontation. That's why simple things such as unbuttoning your coat or uncrossing your arms can make the other person feel less defensive. When you have a rapport with someone, he is much more likely to feel comfortable and open up. Rapport creates trust, allowing you to build a psychological bridge to the person. The conversation is likely to be more positive and you will be much more persuasive. To review, here are a few powerful tips for establishing and building rapport:

Matching posture and movements: If he has one hand in his pocket, you put your hand in yours. If he makes a gesture with his hand, after a moment, you casually make the same gesture.

Matching speech: Try to match his rate of speech. If he's speaking in a slow, relaxed tone, you do the same. If he's speaking quickly, then you speak quickly.

Matching key words: If she is prone to using certain words or phrases, employ them when you speak. For instance, if she says, "I was so uncomfortable with how I was treated," later in the conversation you might say something like, "I know you must have been so uncomfortable with that type of treatment." Make sure that you don't seem to be mimicking her. Obviously copying another's movements is unproductive. A simple reflection of aspects of the person's behavior or speech is enough. This can be a very powerful skill for you, once you become good at it.

 Power Point

In personal instances, where the complaint is directed at you *specifically,* say the following phrase and watch someone's anger dissipate before your eyes: "I couldn't be more sorry. I feel so ashamed." Again, his ego has been damaged and he's seeking to tear you down as well as restore a sense of pride and balance. By acknowledging your own fault you cause him to rebound. Clearly he's gotten through to you because that's exactly what he's been thinking—that you're an idiot. He has nothing left to say. If, at this point, you're still getting flack, go to Chapter 25, Get Anyone to Forgive You for Anything.

Strategy Review

🖊 Say nothing. Just listen. Paraphrase what he's just said. Use "buildup" phrases to reinforce his ego and sense of importance. Ask him what *he* would like you to do.

🖊 While doing the above, establish rapport to help him feel more at ease and comfortable with you.

34

Stop Jealous Behavior in an Instant

It is commonly, though wrongly, believed that in relationships the person most likely to be jealous is someone who has low self-esteem. After all, if someone is confident and feels good about himself, then there is little reason to worry that he will lose his partner to someone else. But it turns out that the relationship between jealousy and a person's self-esteem has been found to be fairly insignificant. Rather, a person is most likely to feel jealous in areas that are especially *relevant to his self-worth.*

In other words, building up your partner's general self-esteem is not usually the answer. He's threatened only in areas that he considers *the basis for his identity.* For example, a doctor may become jealous upon hearing about another doctor who is more proficient than he at a specialized operation. However, he will likely be unmoved upon hearing that Jim, his neighbor, is a better tennis player then he. Why? Because he simply doesn't care. Who he is, how he identifies himself, and how he rates his worth as a human being is by his skill as a surgeon, not as a tennis player.

Let's say that you're a woman who has a wealthy male friend. Your boyfriend is good-looking, smart, caring, and hardworking. But he's insecure about the fact that he doesn't have much money, because to him money is something that is important. Therefore, as far as he's concerned, your friend is more valuable and "better" than he. Your typical strategy might be to build up your boyfriend, and tell him how great he is and how much you care for him; but you will find that ineffective. Telling him that you love him and that he's better-looking and smarter than your friend will do very little to assuage those jealous feelings. *That is not where he's coming from.* Instead you should explain to him why the "quality" in your friend—in this case money—is unimportant to you and his jealousy will simply disappear.

You take the wind out of his jealousy instantly by *downplaying what the other person has that he doesn't*. Your boyfriend values money and hence places a greater value on this guy, so he assumes that you perceive him in the same way. His jealousy is really *envy* of what your friend has that he doesn't.

So it's your friend's qualities—or in this case money—that you need to address, not your boyfriend's qualities. Simply give a rational explanation for why it's not important to you and he'll be fine. For instance, you can say something like, "A true measure of a man is not how much money he has, but who his friends are. While I like my friend, I think that people who flaunt their money do so to compensate for feelings of inadequacy. I like my friend but I feel bad for him." After hearing this, your boyfriend is not going to mind your being friends with him because he no longer feels threatened by the issue of money. If anything, now it's the fact that he *has* money that's comforting, because he believes this is the *very reason* why you find your friend so unappealing.

When you employ this tactic, it is best to do it casually. In this way he is not likely to believe that you are just saying it to make him feel better. A casual approach ensures that *you* believe it and that you want him to know how you feel, and *you're not just saying this to change how he feels.*

Power Point

If you are dealing with someone who is just insanely jealous of *everyone* and *everything*, then you have to handle this a little differently. This person's jealousy is rooted in a deep insecurity and he will "read into" everything that you say or do and conclude that he simply can't trust you. Even the most innocent of situations will be misinterpreted and logic is lost in a sea of unbalanced emotions. While therapy might be in order for this person there is one psychological tactic that will provide temporary relief. He is jealous because he perceives an imbalance in the relationship whereby you are more valuable than he. And he, albeit sometimes unconsciously, believes that it's just a matter of time before you figure this out for yourself. Therefore, *if you become openly jealous about everything that he does,* his perspective should shift dramatically. This is evidenced by the fact that you almost never see a relationship where both people are insanely jealous of the other. This is because one person's jealousy makes the other person "retreat" to more neutral ground.

Strategy Review

✐ A person feels threatened only in areas that he considers *the basis for his identity.* Building up his self-esteem is not the answer. You must downplay the *trait* that he feels he lacks and that others possess. His jealousy is really *envy* of what other people have that he doesn't.

35

How to Get the Best Advice from Anyone

It's been said that advice is something you ask for when you know the answer but wish you didn't. Other times we ask for advice just to confirm our own thinking. So if you do seek it out, have an open mind. Good solid advice from people whom you can trust is invaluable. The problem is that we don't always go about getting good advice the right way.

The first thing to keep in mind is to be wary of asking advice of those who are next to you, metaphorically speaking. Meaning, if you work at a menial job, what do you think your coworker is going to think of your idea of going back to school? Jealousy and envy can creep into the advice and you may not be getting the input that's in your best interest. This is because your coworker's likely justified to himself why he hasn't bettered himself, and will then explain these very same reasons to you. This doesn't mean that it's impossible to get good advice from him, but that it's not likely.

Also, never ask advice from someone who has something at stake or something to lose from your decision. The more objective the person is the greater value you should place on the input. Many people seek advice from friends and family but these people often have an inherent interest in the outcome. This is not to suggest that they would not look out for your best interest, but first, their judgment is clouded by their emotional attachment and second, they may impose what *they would like* for you without considering your wishes.

The reason why we often get poor advice is that it's hard to find a person who always has our best interest at heart, isn't envious in any way, and at no level thinks he knows what's best for you.

And always, always, always, get a second, third, or even fourth opinion about anything that you do. From directions on the road to directions in life, *get feedback from a cross section of people.* This will give you invaluable insight into what you should do. The more people you ask, the greater your perspective. Often a combination of different people's thoughts and ideas is what will work best for you. And you can access anyone's "brain," even if you don't know that person well. There is no better way to get someone's time and attention than to use the phrase: "I'd like to get your advice on something." You might be surprised at the wealth of information available to you when you just ask for it . . . the right way.

 Power Point

There are times when you don't want input from multiple people: in situations where you know that there is a right and there is a wrong, but you're just not clear on which is which. In these instances, you want a single, objective person who is experienced in giving such advice. Find someone who has wisdom in the area in which you seek advice. This is someone who has demonstrated know-how and has the experience to effectively guide you. Don't make the mistake of getting a consensus from several people. Do that in matters of taste and preference where individual opinion is subjective. However, the truth, or what is best for you, is often *objective* and counsel in these areas is best given by someone who is experienced. This is because when there is only one right thing to do, then you need only ask the person who knows.

In addition to specific experience, you should go to someone who listens thoughtfully to what you have to say and *thinks* before offering advice. If he's quick to interrupt without fully hearing the situation, then he is only interested in being heard, not in being helpful.

Strategy Review

✏ Listen with an open mind, not just to confirm what you want to hear.

- Don't ask advice from someone who may be jealous or envious of you or your ideas.
- Don't ask advice from someone who has any type of stake in the outcome—emotional, financial, or otherwise.
- Get feedback from a cross section of people. The more opinions you get the greater perspective you will have.

36

Give the Harshest Criticism Without Ever Offending

When you want to "tell it how it is," but you're worried about bruising his ego or making him feel embarrassed or self-conscious, use this psychological strategy to say your piece without his going to pieces. When you give criticism this way you can be sure you won't offend anyone.

The ego is the pivotal criterion because that is the only part of us that really gets injured. Think of the ego as an image or a projection of how we would like the rest of the world to perceive us. And when this image of ourselves is threatened we become self-conscious. And when it is injured we become hurt (and lash out). The ego is fragile (because it is only an image) and when you deal with others you must seek to protect their egos if you want to spare their feelings. And the *more someone believes that what you're saying is true,* and depending upon how sensitive he is to it, *the more careful you need to be.*

There's a right and wrong way to criticize and how you do it can make all the difference in the world. As you may have experienced, sometimes you're open to criticism and other times the slightest comment can make you feel like crawling under a rock or make you extremely defensive and argumentative. *What* you say, *how* you say it, *where* you say it, and *when* you say it all have a bearing on how your comments are received.

The most important part of this overall strategy has to do with the *timing* of your conversation. The best time to criticize is *when you are removed from the event.* For instance, if you want to have a discussion with your lover on how she can improve her lovemaking skills, don't bring it up while you're in bed five minutes after sex. Discuss it when you are removed from the environment—out for a drive, perhaps, days later.

Being removed from the environment *as well as putting time between the event and your critique* is also significant. Because while you may verbally assure the person that it is no big deal, you don't convey that attitude by speaking up immediately. By waiting a few days you reduce his ego attachment to the situation and he's less sensitive to criticism. But the closer to the event (in both time and proximity) that you criticize, *the more he identifies* with his behavior and the more defensive he will become.

Additionally, when you do criticize, the following *eight psychological factors* will help to ensure that you can be free to voice your objections without worrying about offending him.

1. Without making a big deal about it, let him know you're saying this because you *care*—you care about *him* and your *relationship.*
2. Always criticize in private. Even if you think that it's no big deal, you are best to do it behind closed doors.
3. Preface your criticism with a compliment. For instance, "Bill, you're the most wonderful lover I've ever had, though I was wondering about . . ."
4. Criticize the *act* not the person. In other words instead of saying, "You're annoying when you . . ." it's better to say, "You're great, but on those rare times that [it] happens . . ."
5. Don't assume or insinuate that this is something that he's doing knowingly, consciously, or deliberately. It's best to approach this as something he's doing unwittingly or even unconsciously.
6. Share some of the *responsibility* if you can. Notice I didn't say share the *blame.* This psychological tactic is to make it you and him against this "thing," *not you against him.* In other words, you might say something like, "I should have been more specific when we covered this . . ." This is, of course, more effective than, "I hate it when you . . ."
7. Offer the solution. If there is no answer, then you should never have brought it up in the first place, because it serves no purpose. And if you believe that no matter what you say he will not take your advice, then also don't bring it up. If you do then you

are only serving your own interests and this will not help the situation.

8. Criticism is most effective when you tell him that he is not alone. By conveying that whatever he's done or doing is very common diffuses the impact on the ego—meaning he doesn't take it so personally. And that's really the reason we become so offended—it's because we take it personally.

Strategy Review

🖉 The best time to criticize is when you are *removed* from the event.

🖉 Put *time* between the event and your critique.

🖉 Tell the person that you are mentioning this because you *care*.

🖉 Always criticize in private.

🖉 Preface your criticism with a compliment.

🖉 Criticize the *act* not the person.

🖉 Share some of the *responsibility* if you can.

🖉 Offer the solution.

🖉 Let him know that he is not alone.

37

Get Anyone to Confide in You and Confess Anything

You can gain a person's trust instantly and get anyone to open up and tell you just about anything that you want to know. The ability to gain a person's confidence is simply a matter of following a specific psychological strategy, and is outlined below.

Let's say that you're a police detective, a principal, or a minister—you can establish a trusting relationship within minutes with just about anybody. Here's how you do it. First, if possible and appropriate, tell someone a secret or something personal because this shows that you trust him. But it's important to make him think that he's earned it. Otherwise he'll think you're a crackpot who just spills his guts to anyone. If he feels that you trust him he will be more likely to trust you. Not only does this ingratiate you, but also it enacts the law of reciprocation.

When you tell something about yourself, not only does the other person feel psychologically closer to you, but he *feels a need to reciprocate* by sharing something personal with you. He then begins to open up to you and therein lies the real power behind the tactic. This is a fascinating and highly effective psychological phenomenon that works because once he gives you something—even if it's his opinion—*he trusts you more* than if he *didn't* share this information. The more he shares with you, the closer he feels to you. This paves the way for him to really open up to more personal and private things.

The unconscious interactions at play here are that once someone shares something with you, he trusts you more. The unconscious thought process is, "Why else would I have told you? I must trust you." In order to reduce the feelings produced by the dissonance, he reconciles this conflict by concluding that he must indeed trust you.

If you're speaking with someone who is being tight-lipped with *any* meaningful information, try the following approach. Ask him what he believes about esoteric things like God, or how he feels about reincarnation or abortion, and so on. *He will tell you* because he doesn't consider this information to be a threat because it can't be used against him. He's just opened himself up, however, in a highly personal way. He's shared more than a secret; *he's told you who he is,* and he has bared his consciousness. This is what makes him feel connected to you and more trusting of you.

Interestingly enough, not all secrets are created equal. Our identity—who we are—is most closely linked not to what we do but to what we believe. The gateway to trust is easily entered through this unprotected back door. This type of information is more easily gained because the person is thinking, "What's the harm?" But it creates an unexpected vulnerability and attachment. When he does tell you his views, do not argue or debate the merit of his beliefs. If you "coincidentally" share the same views this will significantly increase your psychological bond. You can also increase his need to tell you by having him focus on his *emotional state.*

This enhancement is based on the following research into support and emotions. *Focusing on how you feel in an unpleasant situation results in a greater need to talk about your feelings.* In this study, FBI trainees took part in an exercise in which they played the role of abducted hostages. Some were told to focus on the *situation,* others on their *emotional state,* and some were given no instructions at all. In this highly stressed situation, *self-focusing on emotions led to increased emotional awareness and a strong desire to seek social support* (Strentz and Auerbach, 1988).

This is in part why women, who are often more in touch with their feelings, usually feel that their mates do not communicate enough or give them the emotional support that they need. By making the person think about his emotions, you unconsciously force him to seek support from you, to open up, and to share. To apply this, simply have the person focus on *how* he feels about the situation, not on the situation itself. This will greatly increase his need to talk about it and to express his concerns and feelings. It makes him actually *need someone to talk to* about anything stressful that is going on in his life.

Keep in mind, too, never to beg. Let him know that your desire to know is not out of curiosity but out of concern. Begging portrays you as someone who's interested in knowing, not in helping.

Finally, if you want specific information about something he's done, when appropriate, offer a *benefit* for telling you. Letting him get it off his chest is okay but not always too effective. Offer concrete help for the situation. If he's done something wrong or he's in trouble let him know that whatever it is you are willing to help in any way that you can. By combining emotional support with a concrete offer to help he will open up to you.

In some instances, if he's done something that he's not proud of, the last obstacle may be his concern about what you will think of him, so let him know that you will not be judgmental and that everybody does things that he is embarrassed about or regrets. Here, too, would be a good time to share some of your little secrets with him that you're not too proud of either.

If he hasn't told you yet, but he's close and just needs a little more prodding, then this next tactic will help him become more comfortable opening up. It forces him to reconcile *why he did* what *he did* and the only way to do that is to conclude that he was justified.

In your conversation, continue to repeat phrases like the ones below, making sure that they contrast *a reason* vs. *no reason.* (a) "You could only do what you did if you felt you had to or why else would you?" (b) "Nobody does things unless he has a reason; only insane people do that. But you're not nuts." (c) "You did it because you knew you had to at the time. It made sense then, so that's why you did it. You do things that make sense, don't you?"

These simple phrases begin to wear down his defenses and he'll seek out confirmation of his actions. Sometimes they will work right away; other times it may take a little while. But if someone keeps hearing such phrases over and over again, he will break, and you will get a confession.

Strategy Review

- Tell him a secret or something personal about what is going on in your life. When someone tells us something about himself, not only do we feel psychologically closer but we feel a need to reciprocate by sharing something personal with him.

- Ask him about his views on something general. When he does tell you, do not argue or debate the merit of his beliefs. If you "coincidentally" share the same views this will significantly increase your psychological bond.

- By having the person focus on his emotions, you unconsciously force him to seek support from you, to open up, and to share. To apply this, have the person focus on *how* he feels about the situation, not on the situation itself.

- If appropriate, offer a *benefit* for telling you. Letting him get it off his chest is okay but not always effective.

- Fear of what you will think of him is often an obstacle. Overcome this by letting him know that you are not judgmental and that we all do things that we're not proud of.

38

How to Handle Any Tough (or Stupid) Questions

Get Anyone to Back Off Instantly and Win Every Argument Every Time

Being skilled in the art of verbal self-defense can be an invaluable asset. We so often get locked into ridiculous arguments and drawn into answering asinine questions. A lot has been written about such dialogues, but the challenge with much of the traditional advice is that it *presumes you are able to have an intelligent, logical, and meaningful conversation with this person.* The reason the conversation has degraded to this point is that you likely can't. Suggesting that *you* take a deep breath and tell *her* that you respect her feelings and so on is just plain bad advice. Because it almost never works when you're talking to an idiot. It sounds good in theory, but if she were interested in a calm and intelligent conversation and exchange of ideas you wouldn't be locked into this argument in the first place. The psychological tactics offered here assume that the line of communication is no longer open to rational thought. Instead, you need to use potent techniques that will quickly and effectively allow you to take control of the conversation and the situation.

Two Biggest Mistakes Almost Everyone Makes

I: The first rule of effective debate, argument, or heated conversation is to *never, ever, get defensive.* The minute you begin to defend yourself against an accusation, you've lost. Now you're fighting uphill. When you do this you are giving credence to what is said and you're arguing with your back against the wall.

Unfortunately, this is what many of us instinctually want to do and have been told to do. But it's wrong. If you've ever watched anyone get defensive, he not only can *appear* guilty but he quickly becomes a verbal punching bag by constantly being on the defensive.

II: The other big mistake we make is to accept the person's premise and argue from that point. For instance someone says to you, "You don't look very good. Why don't you take better care of yourself?" The starting point for the conversation is that you don't look very good. That's not the premise you want to start from because then no matter what you say as to why you do, don't, or how you take care of yourself, you're still operating from a deficit and a disadvantage. For instance, if you say, "Well, that's because I was up all night . . ." then she says, "Why were you up all night? Aren't you able to finish the work?" Now you're in an argument and you're forced to defend yourself.

THE SOLUTION

Since your objective is not to get defensive, you need to go on the offensive. This way you can defend yourself *without getting defensive*. When asked a question that you feel is a cheap shot respond with: "What answer would satisfy you?"

When you ask this question you'll get one of two responses. You may get an "I don't know," in which case you can respond with "Well, if you asked the question and don't know what answer you want, how am I supposed to know?"

The other answer is the one you'll likely get and it will be something specific—but now you've got something to work with. And notice that she's the one answering your questions, *with her back against the wall*. For instance, someone says that you're not old enough to be doing "X." Instead of saying, "Yes, I am because of . . ." (which is defensive, because now she's going to pick apart your reasons), your preferred answer is "How old would you like me to be?" For argument's sake let's say that she says thirty-four. "Well, what about thirty-three, is that too young?" is your answer.

Now the person has to defend what she said instead of you defending yourself!

Here's the best part. When you ask someone to get more specific, it's harder for her to justify her statement and corresponding beliefs. *For example, she now has to define the differences between thirty-three and thirty-four.* No one can do this. Then when she does give an answer, you continue to press her further as to why she feels this way and ask her to be more specific

The strategy here is to *ask her to explain why her premise is right, not why your answer is.* To anyone listening and watching she's going to appear to be very rigid and unyielding because she has to defend herself against her own ideas. And in actuality, *any idea or belief that is reduced to specifics almost always sounds silly* when you try to defend it.

So when you're asked a question, don't get defensive and don't argue from her premise. Ask her a question as to why *she believes* what she does and have her argue her point.

STUPID STATEMENTS

Now what about those times when someone says something stupid about or to you, but not in the form of a question? Any usual attempt to defend yourself will sound like you're justifying the comment and getting way too defensive and upset. Again though, you can turn the tables on someone in a second.

THE SOLUTION

In response to something ridiculous like, "You'd be nothing without me" or "That's so stupid what you did," say, "You don't even believe that's true." Now again, the person has to defend what he's said and you can argue with him about his reasons instead of him arguing with you about yours.

Another great response is "Why would you say something like that?" or "Why are you finding fault with everything? Aren't you at all happy with anything in your life?" You see, just by not getting defensive *you force him to explain himself* and you never have to say the word "I" *because if you don't make it about you then he can't argue with you!*

Turn Any Argument Around

Okay, but what if you're losing the argument, you don't have the facts on your side, and you just want out? Don't worry, this wonderful psychological technique will save you in an instant.

If you don't like the question you're asked, then don't answer it; *answer a different one.* To do this, simply say something such as, "In terms of what?" or "How exactly do you mean?" This forces a person to rephrase the question and you'll answer this new specific question instead of the original one, and all without seeming to have dodged it. For instance, you're asked, "How come all of the workers are complaining about the conditions?" There's no way you can answer that and win. It's like asking somebody if he's still beating his wife. Any answer is a bad one. So ask the other person to clarify her question and answer the new specific question. Here's how the exchange might go:

"How exactly do you mean?"

"Oh, José, Fred, and I think Beth has said that nobody gets long enough lunch breaks." Now *you've got three people* complaining about the lunch hour *instead of every worker complaining* about the conditions. It becomes a much easier question and situation to deal with, but you can still narrow it further and the questioner will begin to seem very argumentative instead of you.

"Lunch breaks?" you answer, and continue. "How long would they like to eat lunch for?" You can see that the wind of her argument dissipates quite quickly. You've managed to answer a new question, put her on the defensive, and force her to get into specifics.

Again, what's very important is that you want to avoid appearing as if you are trying to dodge the question. The technique below is another way to gently shift the focus without being argumentative and allow for a more constructive and useful conversation, all without being defensive. If the above techniques aren't appropriate then use the following:

After being asked a tough question, respond with, "I think what you're really saying is . . ." (and then switch the question). The following illustrates how this is done:

You're told, "I don't think you're capable of running this company." Respond with, "I think what you're really saying is that if I could show you how I can not only cut costs but also increase earnings, you'd be interested, right?" Now that wasn't his question but it implies the motivation behind it. *He is forced to agree* because there would likely be no other reason why you wouldn't be capable of running the company. Now you explain your strategy for increasing sales and you never look back.

You're told, "I don't think you care about this relationship." You say, "I think what you're really saying is that you've been hurt and I need to be able to show you that it will never happen again." Again, now you have something specific to work with. Answering abstract questions intelligently is nearly impossible. Bring it to something clear and specific and then respond. Don't be goaded into responding to a vague statement. You can't win. *Change the question, reduce it to specifics, and then answer.*

Let's take one more example. You're asked, "How could you have screwed up so badly?" You respond with, "If I understand you correctly, I think you really want to know what factors were involved that you may not be aware of." That's not his question, but it's a much easier one to answer.

Take 5

Finally, when you're under the gun and you need time to plan your strategy, use *conversation stoppers*. These are phrases that are *mild trance inducers.* In other words, they cause the listener to zone out temporarily while his brain tries to process the information. Use them when you need to gain control of the conversation or to regroup. They give you some time to collect your thoughts while others temporarily lose their train of thought. As you read them, you'll notice that the syntax is off slightly, and causes the mind to sort of "lock up" for a few seconds while it tries to process the information. This technique is used widely in hypnosis to implant suggestions in the unconscious mind:

"Why are you asking me what you don't know for sure?"
"Do you really believe what you thought you knew?"

"I understand what you're saying; it doesn't make it true."
"If you expected me to believe that, you wouldn't have said it."
"Your question is what you knew it would be, isn't it?"
"Do you believe that you knew what you thought?"
"Are you unaware of what you forgot?"

Strategy Review

- *Never, ever, get defensive.* The minute you try to defend yourself, you've lost.
- Don't automatically accept the person's premise or you may be starting at a disadvantage. Instead gain leverage and ask *him* to explain why he thinks the way he does.
- Don't be goaded into responding to a vague statement. You can't win. *Change the question, reduce it to specifics, and then answer.*
- If you're really at a loss, use the power of hypnosis to gain some time to think and strategize.

39

Just for Parents

Get Your Child to Behave the Right Way, Right Away!

These techniques show you how to get your child to cooperate with you when your parenting skills are really put to the test.

It should be noted here that often hyperactivity and other behavioral problems are rooted in *physiological* causes, *not psychological*. Foods containing caffeine, sugar, or any substance that your child may be allergic to (even something seemingly innocuous such as wheat, rice, or milk) can create a serious psychological imbalance. Remember that small children who have even a few sips of cola can react the same way as an adult drinking two or three cans. Even the most effective parenting skills can be thwarted if your child is incapable of paying attention because he's bouncing off the walls. Never underestimate the power of diet in your child's behavior.

There are essentially two elements for gaining cooperation from your child, or for that matter, any adult. They are giving him the feeling of control, and using emotion-based arguments. The following is an example of how both of these can work either independently or together.

How do you get your child to listen to you? Whether it's a problem at bedtime or not wanting to get dressed, this technique will prove to be highly effective. *Give him a choice.* Make him an active part of the process by giving him a choice that implies cooperation. For instance, instead of saying to a child, "Will you please sit at the table for lunch?" you say "Do you want to sit in the chair facing the TV or would you rather look out the window at the table?" If you give him the *illusion of control* he is much more willing to cooperate; and once he commits himself then he will follow through.

This is true for adults as much as it is for children. Studies show us that prisoners who are able to exercise some control over their environments—by being able to move furniture, control TV sets, and switch the lights on and off—experience less stress and commit less vandalism. Research in this area also overwhelmingly concludes that *workers* given leeway in carrying out tasks and making decisions experience improved morale.

People, and that means children too, need to believe that they have some control over their lives. If they don't, this can develop into what is called *learned helplessness,* characterized by a person's perception that he has no control over repeated bad events or even over routine happenings in his life. This can lead to disruptive behavior and psychological problems. We should say here that giving a child too much leeway, without appropriate boundaries, can also cause major disciplinary problems. Children need parameters and will push as far as they can until they reach them. By not setting appropriate boundaries the child's behavior will reach erratic proportions until he meets with resistance.

The other element is to not try to sway a child with logic. How do you get her to do what's best for her? Translate cold hard facts into something that affects *her* reality. If you want her to brush her teeth, for example, telling her she'll get cavities if she doesn't means nothing. Instead tell her that we brush our teeth so we can enjoy the foods we like. She has no frame of reference for cavities but she certainly does for eating tasty food.

Strategy Review

- Behavioral problems are often rooted in *physiological* causes, *not psychological.* Foods containing caffeine, sugar, or any substance that your child may be allergic to can create a serious psychological imbalance.
- Give your child a feeling of control over what happens in his life. If you give him the *illusion of control* he is much more willing to cooperate and once he commits himself he will follow through.
- Use emotion-based arguments. Translate cold hard facts into something that affects *her* reality.

40

Get Out of Almost Any Physical or Sexual Assault

Smarter Living for Men and Women

Of all the tactics in this book, this may be one that can save more than just your sanity and self-respect, but possibly even your life. To understand the dynamics and application of the psychological techniques, we'll divide these attacks into two categories: sexual assaults and physical assaults.

 Power Point

If your attacker just wants things—your money, wallet, purse, jewelry, or *anything but you,* give it to him! Any of these items can be replaced . . . you cannot. If he just wants "things," then you are lucky.

SEXUAL ASSAULTS: APPLY THESE TECHNIQUES IN ASCENDING ORDER
Please remember that there are no foolproof methods that will work every time in every situation. You need to assess the situation and do whatever makes sense to you at the time. The following will offer you some options and ideas that may prove to be effective, but for more detailed information you are encouraged to call The National Center for Victims of Crime at 800 FYI-CALL.

1. In situations where you and he know each other—you either have a relationship with this person, or you've met before—*pretend to be interested and excited* in what the person is doing. In an at-

tempted rape situation your *only* objective is to get away before you are harmed. This can best be accomplished by letting your attacker *believe* that you do not want to get away. Therefore, *if you initiate or carry through some small degree of affection, he, in his heightened state of arousal, will likely accept your intentions as honest.* Then, when he is vulnerable or you have an opportunity, injure him and/or leave the situation. Remember that if he believes that you are a willing participant he will behave less aggressively and much differently. This will *give you control* over your circumstances.

Sometimes the mistake people make is to resist initially, either verbally, physically, or both. Resist your instinct to defend yourself. If you do not become defensive, then he will not be as aggressive and will move more slowly and carelessly and give you your out.

Remember that your first tactic should be to look for an escape, but if you can't, let him think that this is what you want. Some rapists who know the victim believe that this person wants it, so you don't need to do a lot of convincing. His guard will be down as long as he doesn't think that you want to escape. And when he relaxes his guard, move.

Aside from initiating some small gesture toward physical contact, *smile.* That's right, smile! We've talked often about the power of smiling in this book. This is a universal sign that you are *comfortable* and *accepting* of the situation. Let him see a big, broad, wide, encompassing smile.

Depending on how well you know this person, you may need to provide for a "reasonably logical motivation" for your wanting to have sex with this person. If you are convincing enough, you can try to convince him, too, that it has to be just perfect and that you want a change of venue—to go somewhere where it will be more romantic.

If you don't know your attacker, you can still try to "convince" him of your interest. Assuming you're able to carry on some sort of dialogue, you should tell him that this is your *exact fantasy* and that you want it to be just perfect. *Tell him what to do*—such as lie down, take off your shirt. If he complies then you will have gained some control of the situation. Then, do whatever it takes to either incapacitate him and/or escape. *Note:* You should be aware that if the assault continues, this tactic may be used against you in court. The defense may use your 'overt interest' as an indication that you wished for the encounter to take place.

2. Try to calm your attacker and persuade him not to carry out the attack. Some women have been successful by simply *telling* their attackers not to continue. For this to be effective the woman must speak confidently and assuredly. You should be direct and *clear*. "No! Stop this now."

3. If you are at home, tell him somebody will be back soon. If you are in a more public place, yell, scream, and try to create any type of disturbance.

4. You may be able to turn off the attacker by: repulsing him by vomiting, urinating, belching, and so on; claiming to be sick or have AIDS; pretending to be insane or mentally deranged.

5. Physical self-defense. If you decide to fight, make sure that you are not afraid to inflict serious pain on your attacker. Hit him where it hurts. Eyes, groin, throat, and nose are particularly vulnerable. If you feel that you will be injured and hurt by defending yourself, do not feel guilty. Survival is your ultimate objective. A victim who does not fight back should never feel guilty or ashamed—sometimes it's the smartest thing to do.

 Power Point

If your attacker wants to take you somewhere, *do whatever you can to avoid going with him.* Studies show that once he gets you in a car or away from where you are, your chances of being harmed increase significantly. Scream, punch, kick, and do whatever you need to do to not be taken from where you are. The best defense is a smart offense. If you don't find yourself in these situations, then you will not have to worry about how to get out of them. Be smart, and use caution. You never know who you are dealing with!

PHYSICAL ASSAULTS: FOR MEN AND WOMEN

If you follow these tactics, you can get out of just about any physical assault. Your sole objective is to get out of the situation without being injured. It's smarter to walk away with a bruised ego than a bruised face.

1. Okay, somebody did something to you that you don't appreciate. The problem is you never know who you're talking with. In an age when many people walk around with a weapon and an attitude, you need to be careful. First a word to the wise. If somebody steps on your foot, cuts you off, bumps into you, whatever . . . *let it go!* Did he do it on purpose because he's looking for a fight? Was it an accident? Does he not like you and want to show that he's bigger and stronger than you? Is he trying to prove something to you, himself, or somebody else? You don't always know, and most important, who cares? If you can walk away, *walk away.*

2. If this is happening with someone whom you know and is beginning with verbal abuse, then understand the dynamics here. The person treats you this way because it makes him feel *powerful.* To diffuse his anger, acknowledge his "authority and power." To do this, simply say, "You're right, I'm sorry." Then remove yourself from the situation.

3. If the above isn't working fast enough you can use this tactic. *Become more upset at yourself than the person is.* He is yelling because he wants you to feel the way he does: angry, hurt, frustrated, and *small.* So if you make him believe that you feel worse than he does, he accomplishes nothing more by yelling. When you beat yourself up verbally he has no real motivation to hurt you physically because his ego is being assuaged.

4. There's an old saying: "Never argue with anyone who is crazier than you." Do whatever you can to make him think that you're nuts. Scream, yell, talk to imaginary people, whatever. Here's why this works. He is looking to fight you because he believes that he will be victorious. No matter how angry we get, we rarely pick a fight with someone who we *know* can beat the daylights out of us. If you do what he does not expect then the person will conclude that you are *unpredictable,* capable of anything and may indeed be a threat. He's no longer in control of the situation and, hence, doesn't feel as powerful.

5. If that's not working then *hit first* and *hit hard*. Don't start a fight but if you have no choice, make sure that you finish it. Hit him where it hurts. Eyes, groin, throat, and nose are particularly vulnerable.

Strategy Review

SEXUAL ASSAULTS:

- *Resist initially your inclination to defend yourself* either verbally or physically.
- Try to *calm* your attacker and persuade him not to carry out the attack.
- If you are at home, tell him somebody will be back soon. If you are in a more public place, yell, scream, and try to create any type of disturbance.
- You may be able to turn off the attacker by: repulsing him by vomiting, urinating, belching, and so on; claiming to be sick or have AIDS; pretending to be insane or mentally deranged.
- Physical self-defense. Hit him where it hurts. Eyes, groin, throat, and nose are particularly vulnerable.

PHYSICAL ASSAULTS:

- To diffuse his anger, acknowledge his "authority and power." To do this simply say, "You're right, I'm sorry."
- Become more upset at yourself than the person is and remove his unconscious "incentive" for physical abuse.
- We tend to stay away from people who are crazier then we are. *Act unpredictably.*
- If nothing else works, then be practical. Hit first and hit hard. Hit him where it hurts. Eyes, groin, throat, and nose are particularly vulnerable.

Conclusion

This book offers psychological solutions to correcting problems, not people. For instance, if you find yourself in an abusive relationship, this book will certainly help you to take control of harmful situations, but it won't address the larger issue, which is *why* you are in this relationship. If people are taking advantage of you, then this book will help you to see through them, but it won't help you to choose your friends better. Additionally, if you act without thinking and need someone to forgive you, this book will also help you to be forgiven. But if you are constantly apologizing for things you've done, it won't help you to think more about the ramifications of what you do and say and how that can hurt someone.

If you find yourself on the receiving end of a jealous partner, you can easily quash the jealousy with a single psychological technique that takes all of about thirty seconds. But it won't help you to reevaluate the relationship or to examine the root of your partner's jealousy.

This is like no other self-help book because it makes life easy without much effort. You simply plug in the psychological technique and the problem is solved. But if you continue to find yourself in these difficult situations, I would encourage you to look more closely at your choices in life.

In compiling these tactics, every attempt was made to instill a sense of morality, using the barometer of "the greater good" for all concerned. For example, lying to protect someone from embarrassment or hurt feelings is likely to be beneficial to everyone. And using deception is acceptable if it will keep *you* from being harmed or taken advantage of. These, however, are not always black-and-white issues, so appreciation goes to my friend Rabbi Henry Harris for helping me to clarify certain points of morality. If, however, these techniques seem to veer from this "higher ground," please know that it is not a reflection of Rabbi Harris's wisdom, but rather a departure to effectively illustrate a point.

You will notice that you feel much better about yourself and life in general. This is because much of our inner turmoil and frustration comes from our inability to deal effectively with people and to handle difficult situations and conflicts. So as you begin to apply these techniques, you'll find new doors opening up for you as you gain a greater sense of who you are and what you are capable of. And this renewed self-image can help you to shape your future into anything that *you* choose. Instead of being a victim of the tides, you will be able to direct your destiny and take full advantage of life's greatest gift—*free will.*

This book was written to help give you a sense of empowerment and control over your life. But with that control comes an incredible, tremendous opportunity.

It can—if you will let it—allow you to benefit others in ways you never could have before. When things in our own life are not going well, it can be hard to extend a helping hand to others. When you're in control, you're accomplishing more and feeling terrific about yourself and about your life. Empowering others will allow you to take your personal growth to an entirely new level.

Enjoy your new life.

Bibliography

Aronson, E., B. Willerman, and J. Floyd (1966). The effect of a pratfall on increasing interpersonal attractiveness. *Psychonomic Science*, 4.

Asch, S. E. (1946). Forming impressions of personalities. *Journal of Abnormal and Social Psychology*, 41.

Carlsmith, J. M., and A. E. Gross (1969). Some effects of guilt on compliance. *Journal of Personality and Social Psychology*, 11.

Cialdini, R. B., B. L. Green, and A. J. Rusch (1992). When tactical pronouncement of change becomes real change. The case of reciprocal persuasion. *Journal of Personality and Social Psychology*, 6.

Curtis, R. C., and K. Miller (1986). Believing another likes or dislikes you: Behaviors making the beliefs come true. *Journal of Personality and Social Psychology*, 51.

Dutton, D. G., and A. P. Aron (1974). Some evidence for heightened sexual attraction under conditions of high anxiety. *Journal of Personality and Social Psychology*, 30.

——— (1989). Romantic attraction and generalized liking for others who are sources of conflict-based arousal. *Canadian Journal of Behavioral Science*, 21.

Frank M. G., and T. Gilovich (1998). The dark side of self and social perception: Black uniforms and aggression in professional sports. *Journal of Personality and Social Psychology*, 54.

Freedman, J. L., and S. C. Fraser (1966). Compliance without pressure: The foot-in-the-door technique. *Journal of Personality and Social Psychology*, 4.

Higgins, E. T., W. S. Rholes, and C. R. Jones (1977). Category accessibility and impression formation. *Journal of Experimental Social Psychology*, 13.

Kahneman, D., and J. Snell (1992). Predicting a change in taste: Do people know what they will like? *Journal of Behavioral Decision Making*, 5.

Kellerman, J., J. Lewis, and J. D. Laird (1989). Looking and loving: The effects of mutual gaze on feelings of romantic love. *Journal of Research in Personality*, 23.

Kelley, H. H. (1950). The warm-cold variable in first impressions of persons. *Journal of Personality*, 18.

Kleinke, C. L., F. B. Meeker, and R. A. Staneski (1986). Preference for opening lines: Comparing ratings by men and women. *Sex Roles*, 15.

Langer, E., A. Blank, and B. Chanowitz (1978). The mindlessness of ostensibly thoughtful action: The role of "placebic" information in interpersonal interaction. *Journal of Personality and Social Psychology*, 36.

Leventhal, H., R. Singer, and S. Jones (1965). The effects of fear and specificity of recommendation upon attitudes and behavior. *Journal of Personality and Social Psychology*, 2.

Lipsitz, A., K. Kallmeyer, M. Ferguson, and A. Abas (1989). Counting on blood donors: Increasing the impact of reminder calls. *Journal of Applied Social Pscyhology*, 19.

Loftus, E. F. (1979). *Eyewitness Testimony*. Cambridge, Mass.: Harvard University Press.

Michaels, J. W., J. M. Blommel, R. M. Brocato, R. A. Linkous, and J. S. Rowe (1982). Social facilitation and inhibition in a natural setting. *Replications in Social Psychology*, 2.

Milliman, R. (1982). Using background music to affect the behavior of supermarket shoppers. *Journal of Marketing*, 46.

Montepare, J. M., and L. Zebrowitz-McArthur (1988). Impressions of people created by age-related qualities of their gaits. *Journal of Personality and Social Psychology*, 54.

Moreland, R. L., and R. B. Zajonc (1982). Exposure effects in person perception: Familiarity, similarity, and attraction. *Journal of Experimental Social Psychology*, 18.

Petty, R. E., J. T. Cacioppo, and R. Goldman (1981). Personal involvement as a determinant of argument-based persuasion. *Journal of Personality and Social Psychology*, 41.

Rhodewalt, F., and J. Davison, Jr. (1983). Reactance and the coronary-prone behavior pattern: The role of self-attribution in response to reduced behavioral freedom. *Journal of Personality and Social Psychology*, 44.

Roballey, T. C., C. McGreevy, R. R. Rongo, M. L. Schwantes, P. J. Steger, M. A. Wininger, and E. B. Gardner (1985). The effect of music on eating behavior. *Bulletin of the Psychonomic Society*, 23.

Ross, L., and S. M. Samuels (1993). The predictive power of personal reputation versus labels and construal in the Prisoner's Dilemma game. Unpublished manuscript, Stanford University.

Sarason, I. G., B. R. Sarason, G. R. Pierce, E. N. Shearin, and M. H. Sayers (1991). A social learning approach to increasing blood donations. *Journal of Applied Social Psychology*, 21.

Shapiro, D. R., E. H. Buttner, and B. Barry (1992). Explanations: What factors enhance their perceived inadequacy? *Organizational Behavior and Human Decision Processes*, 1.

Strentz, T., and S. M. Auerbach (1988). Adjustment to the stress of simulated captivity: Effects of emotion-focused versus problem-focused preparation on hostages differing in locus of control. *Journal of Personality and Social Psychology*, 55.

Vroom, V. H., and P. W. Yetton (1973). *Leadership and Decision-making*. Pittsburgh: University of Pittsburgh Press.

Walster Hatfield, E. (1965). The effect of self-esteem on romantic liking. *Journal of Experimental Social Psychology*, 1.

Weiner, B., J. Amirkhan, V. S. Folkes, and J. A. Verette (1987). An attributional analysis of excuse giving: Studies of a naïve theory of emotion. *Journal of Personality and Social Psychology*, 52.

Wing, R. L. (1986). *The Tao of Power.* New York: Doubleday.

Zimbardo, P. G. (1970). The human choice: Individuation, reason, and order versus deindividuation, impulse, and chaos. In W. J. Arnold and D. Levine, eds. (1969), *Nebraska Symposium on Motivation,* 17. Lincoln: University of Nebraska Press.

About the Author

DAVID J. LIEBERMAN, Ph.D., whose books have been translated into eleven languages, is an internationally renowned leader in the field of human behavior. He has appeared on more than two hundred programs and is a frequent guest expert on national television and radio shows such as *The Today Show,* National Public Radio, *The View,* PBS, *The Montel Williams Show,* and A&E. Dr. Lieberman holds a Ph.D. in psychology and is the creator of Neural-Dynamic Analysis, a revolutionary short-term therapy. He is a sought-after speaker, lecturer, and consultant. Techniques based on his work have led to groundbreaking advancements in numerous fields and are used by governments, corporations, and professionals in more than twenty-five countries. He lives in New York City.

READ DR. LIEBERMAN'S INTERNATIONALLY ACCLAIMED BOOK

TRANSLATED INTO 11 LANGUAGES

INSTANT ANALYSIS

In 1997 INSTANT ANALYSIS captured worldwide attention. *ABC World News Now* led the charge when they announced, "Before rushing into therapy, consider this method for leading an examined life." And PBS put it best when they succinctly said, *"Instant Analysis says it all."*

Why do I feel the need to arrive early?   Why do I need to have the TV or radio on when I'm alone?
Why do some people annoy me so easily?   Why am I so absentminded?
Why am I so easily discouraged?
Why do I take so long to make simple decisions?   Why am I so reluctant to plan for my future?
Why do I put off things that would only take a few minutes to do?   Why do I keep people waiting?
Why do I have such difficulty disciplining myself?
Why do I feel alone even when I'm around people?
Why do I rarely get a full tank of gas and then let it run on fumes before refueling?
Why do I misplace my keys, papers, and just about everything?
Why do I complicate the simplest things?
Why am I so easily distracted?   Why do I think about acting totally inappropriately in public?
Why do I enjoy being angry?   Why do I do favors for people I don't even like?
Why am I so hard on myself?   Why am I so competitive?
Why do I feel the need to control others?
Why do I secretly hope other people will fail?   Why do I obsess over the littlest, stupidest things?
Why do I feel that something bad will happen if something good happens?
Why do I look at my watch to see if I'm hungry or tired?
Why do I have trouble asking people for help?
Why do I attract the wrong type of person and stay in unhealthy relationships?
Why do I enjoy gossiping so much?   Why do I enjoy hearing the confessions of others?
Why am I plagued by self-doubt?   Why do compliments and praise make me uncomfortable?
Why do I feel guilty for things beyond my control?
Why do I apologize even when it's not my fault?
Why am I so superstitious?   Why am I so concerned about the opinions of other people?
Why don't I assert myself when I really need to?
Why do I feel as if nothing will ever make me happy?
Why am I so quick to judge other people?
Why don't I do the things that I know would make me happy?
Why do I worry about things that will never happen or that I have no control over?
Why do I do something halfway when I know I'll just have to do it over again?
Why do I undermine my own efforts?   Why do I eat when I'm not hungry?
Why am I obsessed with my appearance?   Why am I so sensitive to rejection?
Why can I take on the world some days, and other days I can barely get out of bed?
Why do I do such terrible things even though I'm a good person?   Why am I so paranoid?
Why do I feel nobody really knows or understands me?
Why do I eat foods that I know will make me sick?

UNDERSTAND YOURSELF AND OTHERS . . . *IN AN INSTANT*

Visit us at <u>www.InstantAnalysis.com</u>

READ DR. LIEBERMAN'S
PHENOMENAL *New York Times* BESTSELLER

NEVER

Are your kids using drugs?

BE

Is your partner stealing?

LIED TO

Is your spouse having an affair?

AGAIN

Get the Truth in 5 Minutes or Less in <u>Any</u> Conversation or Situation

---

"A fascinating book."—**National Public Radio**

"**If you want to find out whether your boyfriend is cheating, your boss is getting away with murder, or the life-insurance salesman is playing you for a fool, read on.**"—*Cosmopolitan*

"**You don't have to be a pro to pull this stuff off. . . . Even I learned how to do it, and that's saying something. . . . This stuff really works.**"
—**Jeff Rossen, in a Special Report for Fox TV**

"**Don't lie to David Lieberman.**"—*The New York Times*

"**This book can change your life. Best of all it's easy to read and you can apply the [techniques] instantly.**"
—**Dr. Warner Chen, Faculty Fellow at Harvard University**

How many times have you been manipulated or taken advantage of by someone's lies? Are you tired of being deceived, tricked, and fooled? David J. Lieberman shows you how to stop the lies and uncover the truth—in *any* conversation or situation. In a simple, user-friendly format, Dr. Lieberman gives you the tools to determine, with uncanny accuracy, if you are being lied to.

Plus, utilizing newly developed techniques in hypnosis and psycholinguistics, this book also shows you how to easily influence anyone to tell the truth—*within minutes*.

Visit us at <u>www.Truth123.com</u>

AVAILABLE IN EARLY 2002

DAVID LIEBERMAN'S NEXT BOOK

MAKE PEACE
WITH ANYONE

*Breakthrough Strategies to Quickly End
Any Conflict, Feud, or Estrangement*

A Peek Inside His Latest . . .

CONTENTS

PART ONE
The Cause of All Arguments, Conflicts, Feuds, and Estrangements

PART TWO
The Solution to All Arguments, Conflicts, Feuds, and Estrangements

SECTION I: KEEPING SPARKS FROM BECOMING FLAMES: PUT OUT THE FIRE BEFORE IT EVEN BEGINS BY HANDLING DIFFICULT PEOPLE, CONVERSATIONS, AND SITUATIONS THE BEST WAY, RIGHT AWAY

SECTION V: THERE'S NO REASON WE SHOULDN'T BE TALKING. THE SITUATION JUST GOT OUT OF HAND AND NOW I WANT TO MAKE THINGS GOOD, AGAIN

SECTION VI: YOU CAN BE THE GREAT PEACE MAKER. END ANY ESTRANGEMENT, CONFLICT, OR FEUD. WHEN NOBODY'S TALKING—WHETHER IT'S BEEN TWENTY MINUTES OR TWENTY YEARS—PUT THE PAST IN THE PAST AND BRING PEOPLE TOGETHER

ADDITIONAL INFORMATION

Dr. Lieberman offers special programs, training, and
workshops in the United States and throughout
the world. Please send your request for
information to the following contact address.
All inquiries must be on official
government or corporate letterhead.

Lieberman & Associates
PO Box 241
Greenvale, NY 11548

www.Truth123.com